P9-CAO-412

READY, BLAME, FIRE!

Myths & Misses in Marketing

Ira Blumenthal

Griffin Publishing Group
Glendale, California

Editorial Statement

In the interest of brevity and unencumbered prose, the editor has chosen to use the standard English form of address. This usage is not meant to suggest that the content of this book, both in its references and to whom it is addressed, is intended as restrictive or exclusive regarding any individual or group of individuals, whether by gender, race, age, or any other means that might be considered discriminatory.

Chairman: Daniel R. Wilson
Publisher: Robert Howland
Director of Operations: Robin Howland
Managing Editor: Marjorie L. Marks
Book Design: Mark M. Dodge
Cover Design: M^2 Graphics
Back Cover Photograph: Barry W. Alsobrook

10 9 8 7 6 5 4 3 2 1
ISBN 1-882180-95-X

Griffin Publishing Group
544 Colorado Street
Glendale, California 91204

Telephone: (818) 244-1470   Fax: (818) 244-7408

Manufactured in the United States of America

ACKNOWLEDGMENTS

I did it. I finally stopped talking about this book and wrote it. It was painful. It was tedious. It was a virtual birthing process.

After conducting hundreds of client meetings, facilitating many seminars and workshops, writing more articles and guest editorials than I care to remember, as well as delivering hundreds and hundreds of speeches....I finally put ideas, words, sentences, paragraphs and chapters on paper and finished the book I've talked about for years. Having laughed at the extensive, effusive Academy Award recipient acknowledgments for decades, I'm not going to fall prey to thanking the producers, directors, sound people, grips (whatever a "grip" is), lighting specialists, hairdressers and the like.

I'm simply going to acknowledge a handful of people who have made a difference in my life. Although each may not necessarily have contributed to the writing of my book, they have each contributed to the writing of my life. For that, I'm eternally grateful.

Thank you, **Kim**, for being my lover, my lady, my luck and my life. Redhead, you should write a book about "partnership" because you're clearly the expert. Thanks for saving me. We made it through the rain! TT, FF, ILU.

Thank you to my children, **Sharon, Julie, Eric, Jeffrey** and **Ryan.** Through each of you, I learned that earning a life is far more important than earning a living. Remember, care and dare to make a difference!

Thank you to my parents, **Bea** and **Larry Blumenthal**, for your confidence, support and legendary love.

Thank you brother **Don**. We've come a long way from 437 Atlantic Avenue. You're the best at "being there."

Thank you **Pat** and **Bill Burgess** for cheese grits, golf tips, as well as lots of good counsel and support over the years.

Thank you **Paul Bodner**. "The best mirror is an old friend," and you're the best at being a best friend. T'us!

Thank you **Cathy Jones** and **Geoff Medeiros** for your loyalty, dedication, commitment, hard work and great voicemails.

Thanks also goes out to the gang at **Coca-Cola USA** for their confidence in my work and counsel; **John Daschler** for the many opportunities; **Dr. David Schoenstadt** for teaching me how to be an entrepreneur and bringing me into the world of pro sports management; **Bob Dylan** for the blast of harmonica spray in my face while onstage in Boston, bringing out the poet in me; **Tom Sullivan** for "seeing" promise in my speaking abilities and for getting my foot in the door of the Washington Speakers Bureau; **"Arthur"** for teaching me to love Rolls Royces; **Steve Prefontaine** for reintroducing me to the concept of "Forever Young!"....**Zsa Zsa Gabor** for making life interesting, to say the least....and to all the many teachers, mentors, coaches, associates, competitors and friends from business, education, sports and literature—thanks for the memories. I also want to acknowledge the loving and learning received from friends and neighbors in all the special neighborhoods: Williamsburg Estates, The Coves, Landen, The Meadows, Riverwoods and Brookstone.

Thanks!

Dedication

To my wife, **Kimberly Lain**, who has always been "the wind beneath my wings," and to the greatest group of children ever assembled in one family....

Sharon, Julie, Eric, Jeffrey and **Ryan**.

◇

CONTENTS

EXPLORING THE MYTHS & MISSES IN BUSINESS & MARKETING

PROLOGUE

An old man and his grandson were walking along a river bank kicking dirt, whistling happy tunes, skipping stones and just generally enjoying each other's company.

While sitting to rest for a few minutes on a fallen tree, the old man said to the twelve-year-old, "Ryan Scott, let's build a bridge."

Surprised, young Ryan asked, "Grandpa, why would we even want to build a bridge? What would be the point? Why?"

The grandfather responded, "Everything has a point. This is a fine wide spot in the river to build a bridge. It will be great fun."

Ryan still didn't understand. Puzzled, he again questioned his grandfather, "I'm confused. Why build a bridge? It might be fun, but it's also going to be really hard work, grandpa."

His grandfather now insisted, "Enough! No more talk. Let's just get up and build us a bridge, son. Gather up small logs and branches. Pile them over here. I'll find some large rocks for a foundation. It'll be great. Let me have that rope in your backpack."

Ever respectful, Ryan stopped his questioning, at least for the moment, and he and his grandfather started bridge-building.

The sun was hot and the two worked very hard.

Hours later, very tired, the young boy couldn't stand it any longer and just had to ask his grandfather one more time, "Grandpa, why are we doing this? You and I have walked along this riverbank many times. We both know that about a mile or two down the river there's a place where the banks come together and almost touch. We've stepped across the banks at that thin point in the river a hundred times. Why are we killing ourselves building this bridge? I'm tired. I'm confused."

The grandfather smiled, hugged his grandson and softly said, "Ryan, please help me build the bridge. Trust me, it's the right thing to do. Just trust me."

Ryan couldn't put his finger on it, but there was something in the old man's tone of voice and something in his smile that gave Ryan new energy. He smiled back, nodded his head in agreement and continued working.

The man and boy worked at an incredibly exhausting pace trying desperately to build their bridge before sunset.

After clearing the land around the river bank, they lifted rock, pulled brush, dragged huge logs and slowly but surely, secured each component piece into a primitive, but usable, expansion bridge.

They were both absolutely exhausted—weary beyond belief, but they finished building the bridge. And a fine little bridge it was.

After munching on some snacks and drinking lots of water, they were ready to head home.

Staring at the masterpiece that he and his grandfather had built, as tired as he was, Ryan was energized by their handiwork and in an upbeat manner, called out to his grandfather,

"C'mon grandpa, let's cross our new bridge and head home. Mom won't believe what we've done. It's really cool. We did it! We did it!"

"Wait a minute, Ryan," the old man said, "Let's not take the bridge across the river. You know, all we really have to do is walk down that path alongside the river a mile or two....you know, where the river gets real thin....there we can hop across the river like we've always done. Forget the bridge. Start marching, pal."

Ryan Scott was shocked. Absolutely, positively baffled beyond belief, he responded, "Grandpa, you know I love you. You also know that if you ask me to do something—you know, like take the trash out or walk the dog or mow the lawn or maybe even build a bridge—I'd do it. But I'm really confused. Why did we work all day long building a bridge for us to use, then not use it when it's time to cross the river and head home!"

The old man smiled, put his arm around Ryan's shoulder and told him, "Son, we didn't build this bridge for our own use. Men don't build bridges so they can use them themselves. They build them for those who follow. This bridge isn't for us, Ryan. We built it for those who follow to use, for those who seek a way to cross the river. That's the whole idea of bridge-building."

Though bewildered and surprised, Ryan smiled, shrugged his shoulders and gave his grandfather a look that only a twelve-year-old could give. Then he and his grandfather continued walking again along the riverbank kicking dirt, whistling happy tunes, skimming stones and just generally enjoying each other's company.

Every seasoned business professional has a responsibility to *build bridges for those who follow.*

After two-and-a-half fun-filled, fast-paced, high-energy decades in the wild, wacky, yet wonderful world of business development, I decided it was time to build a bridge. Names like "Brooklyn," "London," "Golden Gate" and "George Washington" were already taken; therefore, I decided to name my bridge *Ready, Blame, Fire!*

In my career as both a corporate executive and a business consultant, I've fallen prey to believing many of the marketing myths presented in this book. I've also forgotten about the wonderful learning to be derived from studying companies that have experienced incredible marketing misses.

This book, this bridge if you will, spans lots of years, lots of learning and lots of experience. It was written to help business travelers bridge the gap between good and great, between yesterday and today and also between failure and success.

By offering the ideas, information, actionable data, tons of examples, resources, education and motivation for growing forward, *Ready, Blame, Fire!* is designed as an expansion bridge dedicated to expanding its readers' minds. Answering questions as well as questioning answers, I built this bridge *for those who follow.*

I hope it makes a difference!

Ira Blumenthal
3:31 a.m., 5 January 1998

INTRODUCTION

Folksinger and futurist, Bob Dylan, wrote:

> "...there's a battle outside
> And it is ragin'.
> It'll soon shake your windows
> And rattle your walls
> For the times they are a-changin'..."[1]

———— ◇ ————

Change is inevitable. Growth is optional.

———— ◇ ————

But change isn't new. What's new is the incredible speed of change!

One thing's for certain: In times of fast-paced change, someone always emerges as the leader—simply because either they adapted and adjusted well to change or they made other changes.

Leaders adapt, adjust and perform. Leadership is not about position. It's about performance, especially in times of transition.

———— ◇ ————

There are only three things one can do with change: Ignore it, react to it, or make other changes.

———— ◇ ————

I, for one, believe in the "make-other-changes" choice. Whether we call it embracing change, being a change catalyst, striving to be a Paradigm Pioneer®[2] or any other descriptive phrase, the true masters of change survive and invariably thrive in our wacky world of dizzy busyness and business.

———— ◇ ————

Industries, companies and careers move from distinction to extinction because of their inability to cope with change.

———— ◇ ————

Dylan continued:

The line it is drawn.
The curse it is cast...
And the first one now
Will later be last
For the times they are a-changin'.

It is truly bizarre that so many activities and institutions in business are left unchallenged. Rules are rarely questioned, yet they are often revered and respected as the way to wealth.

You see, the brontosaurus no longer stalks the planet—for one reason: It couldn't adapt and adjust.

What happened to Eastern Airlines, W.T. Grant, Howard Johnson's, Euro-Disney, Avon Products, the Union Pacific Railroad and other corporate dinosaurs? Some are ailing, some are failing, some are gone and some have even hit the *comeback trail.*

Whatever happened to rotary phones, newspaper boys, doctors who make house calls, elevator operators, bottle openers, girdles, enclosed telephone booths, roller skate keys (or even roller skates), carbon paper and more?

They're either going or gone.

Things change!

Yet, because many companies and industries have lacked vision and ignored change, they contributed to their own demise and/or extinction.

In his wonderful book, *Paradigms: The Business of Discovering the Future*[2] futurist Joel Barker asserted, "When a paradigm shifts, everyone goes back to zero."

That's exciting to some, scary to others.

Too often, contemporary managers *believe* their products and programs are *ready* and pull the trigger on the initiative, only to find failure, then *blame* anyone and anything remotely associated with the plan, then *fire* the innocent to protect the guilty. Hence, *Ready, Blame, Fire!*

——— ◇ ———

In other words, with every new change, every
brand new day, every "paradigm shift"....
everyone goes back to zero.

——— ◇ ———

Sadly, many business executives and stakeholders find fault and place blame as opposed to accepting or appropriately assigning responsibility for action (or more accurately, inaction). If only they did their homework...

Education is the key. Education is also the primary objective of this book. In short, *Ready, Blame, Fire!* revisits many old rules that perhaps are no longer relevant and that have become "myths." In addition, the book also presents case study illustrations of corporate "misses" that should offer readers ideas, information and education that can be directly applied to their own future business initiatives.

Those who still hold sacred myths such as "bigger is better" and "the first one 'in' wins," might change their viewpoint when reading about Xerox, General Motors, IBM, Apple Computers, Woolworth, Lucky Strike, "New" Coke and a boatload of the other "misses" presented in each chapter that follows.

But remember, books represent only a small piece of the educational process. Ongoing education is an absolute must. When you're through learning, you're through!

In fact, with the fast-paced high-tech communication capabilities that our world possesses, success will not remain only in the hands of the *learned*. The winners will be those who are constantly *learning*.

Continuous education and commitment to learning and an obsession with continuous improvement are vital if one expects to achieve success. Businesses and individuals must stay on top of the information and data or fall to the bottom of the heap. Staying on top usually requires exercising new behaviors and trying new things. Agents of change and those who embrace change typically stay on top. After all, the company (or career, for that matter) that is at the top of the mountain didn't fall there.

Also, the reality is that progress does *not* come through a more-of-the-same attitude. Axioms, rules (myths, if you will) that once were special and important may now have lost their relevancy.

RULES COME AND GO

Companies, products and careers also come and go. Books of business history are filled with stories about the "misses."

Reviewing major misses and past failures provides the link to future success. The key to growth is continuous improvement, to become better at what you do.

The adage, "knowledge is power," is especially true today, when knowledge is the primary means of creating economic value. We have gone from an economy that once moved by BTUs to one that now moves by brain power. Information is fast becoming our most important resource. As a result, the necessity of harnessing brain power and applying knowledge has become vital to success.

Those companies and individuals who focus their business-building efforts on knowledge—you know, ideas, information and actionable data—will win and will surely be better off than everybody else, *if* they apply that knowledge energetically and effectively.

Obviously, somebody has to be better than everybody else. Someone, some company, some product and some program invariably wins, and usually that "win" occurs through an ongoing commitment to learning, to challenging conventional wisdom and to looking at the world differently. After all, most great works of art, industry and science are the result of individuals who looked at the world in a different, original way.

This book is about change, about adaptation, about effectively applying knowledge and about winning.

It is also about looking at the world differently and questioning those old rules (which have become myths) that represent the way things have always been done and seen.

It seems to me that the dying words, the very last words, mind you, of each corporate leader who went down with a sinking company ship likely were: "This is *not* the way we've always done it!"

Still, you get only one result when you do things the way they've always been done, which is *more of the same!* The results of more of the same frequently are simply not acceptable.

There's a lot to be said about disturbing the peace as a formula for growth (and survival).

Still, I always find it ironic, if not silly, that many business people react to new stimuli and *disturbances,* such as out-of-the-box ideas and new ways of doing things, with an almost arrogant negativism. You see, ideas are not considered innovative until the general populace agrees that the new methodology and new-fangled programs are important and worthy of mainstream acceptance.

I have found the following, as absurd as it may seem, to be representative of responses to new or out-of-the-box ideas.

1. Many people, especially the complacent ones, claim that the new idea is simply not sound: "It's not good. It's not true. What a waste!" they say—usually with great conviction.

2. Time passes and the idea seemingly works. Still there's reluctance and negativity. We're likely to hear, "Okay, okay, so maybe it's true. Maybe it works. Maybe it's a good thing. However, it's not very important—not very important at all. Don't waste your time and money on it."

3. More time passes and the idea proves to be productive and seemingly works well. Proving its worth everyday, more and more people are becoming believers in the new idea, product, program or process. Yet the stubborn and the stoical still have reservations. Although they will likely alter their original position somewhat, they usually don't move much. A typical response would be: "Fine, it's proving to be pretty good. Surprise, surprise... it's actually working well. I think the idea has merit for others, however, our situation is such that it just doesn't fit here. We'd never go for it!"

4. Well, eventually lots of time passes and, as one would expect, those who were once cynical have become important program supporters (probably because they had no choice). Oftentimes, ironically enough, they might even try to take credit for the idea and very well be heard backtracking to the effect of, "C'mon now...this was a 'no

brainer!' I believed in it from the beginning. It's real, it's important and I'm proud to say I was one of its early champions. It's wonderful!"

Incredible responses, no? Typical flow of responses? Yes!

It takes courage and cunning to have an open mind. It takes boldness to consider new ideas and new ways of looking at business. Whether you call it vision or imagination, being open-minded is vital for success. In fact, Albert Einstein once said, "Imagination is more important than knowledge."

This book was written to offer open-minded readers ideas and information related to great business myths and terrific (if not horrific) marketing misses. This book is designed to help businesses (and careers) go, but most importantly, to *grow* forward positively, productively and successfully.

This book also was written to explore the proverbial rules. What rules are still relevant? What rules make no sense anymore? What rules should be challenged and what rules should be protected and revered?

Again, virtually every great work of art, industry, medicine, science, etc. came about because someone looked at the world differently and challenged some tried-and-true rule.

Roger von Oech pointed out in his book, *A Whack On The Side Of The Head*,[3] that rules often outlive the purpose for which they were intended. The typewriter keyboard, for instance, was originally positioned with its letters in an illogical sequence in order to slow down typists (to facilitate higher quality) and to keep the key hammers from hitting each other. Even though new forms of typewriters (i.e., computer keyboards) automatically correct errors and have the capacity for high-speed key clicking, the keyboards still use the same letter configuration. Why? It's simple. It's the rule! (And it would require relearning on a wide scale.)

———— ◇ ————

Challenging conventional wisdom through ideas, information, alternative viewpoints and historical perspectives is vital for growth.

———— ◇ ————

This book is focused on growth.

This book also is focused on seeing things clearly. Frequently, it is just as important to understand what something *is* as what it *is not*.

Blind author-philosopher Helen Keller showed great insight when she said:

> I have walked with people whose eyes are full of light but who see nothing in sea or sky, nothing in city streets, nothing in books. It is far better to sail forever in the night of blindness with sense and feeling and mind, than to be content with the mere act of seeing. The only lightless dark is the night of darkness that comes in ignorance and insensibility.

Working diligently to avoid "ignorance and insensibility," as well as challenging longtime trusted rules ("myths") and learning from business blunders ("misses"), can be invaluable for the growth of careers, companies and products.

O.P.E.N., in "IraSpeak," stands for Objectives, Plan, Expectations and Need. Since every book needs an "open," mine follows.

My **objectives,** short and sweet, are to present ideas, convey information, put forth insight, facilitate education, shake up some viewpoints, challenge conventional wisdom, stimulate thinking and motivate you into dynamic action.

My **plan** is to teach by example...focusing on many of the trusted, yet frequently ludicrous, myths and the incredible, history-making misses in the world of business development. Each myth is refuted, then refined...each selected miss is resurrected, then reshaped—simply and succinctly.

"Re" is the prefix of importance in this book (and in business-building).

For instance, consider the power of words such as "redefining," "re-establishing," "reinventing," "reinvigorating," "remarketing," "repositioning," "reshaping," etc.

—— ◇ ——
We're in an age that demands "re"
—— ◇ ——

In terms of **expectations,** you can expect rapid-fire ideas, lots of energy and unbridled passion. You can also expect examples and anecdotes to support each premise. There are lots of fresh, new ideas and some out-of-the-box suggestions as well.

———— ◇ ————
**The mind is like a parachute.
It only works when it's open.**

———— ◇ ————

Finally, there is the **need.** You, your industry, your company, your product line and your career *need* to effectively execute new (or improved) strategies and tactics if you commit to pursuing growth in these complex, highly competitive, tumultuous times.

In short, this book was written to make a difference in some way, whether large or small. Making a difference—isn't that the reason we have all been put on this planet?

Distinction or *extinction* are real possibilities for careers, companies and products. Yet, as words and concepts, *distinction* and *extinction* will forever remain miles apart. Their divergence is comparable to the relationship between "lightning" and "lightning bug"—they have absolutely no similarities and nothing in common.

If I can offer you ideas, information, education, actionable data, real life examples and motivation to help you achieve and maintain distinction, I will be thrilled. By the same token, if I can provide insight and direction that might help you avoid extinction, that, too, will be wonderful.

When dealing with distinction or extinction, there's no middle ground. It's simple. Learn, adapt and change....or become a sorry statistic.

In short, my objective is to provide value and make a difference.

Read on. Enjoy. Grow forward!

Challenge the Myths of Your Own Conventional Wisdom...

INTRODUCTION HIGHLIGHTS

- Change is inevitable. Growth is optional.
- Change isn't new. What's new is the incredible speed of change!
- Leadership is not about position. It's about performance.
- There are only three things one can do with change: Ignore it, react to it, or make other changes.

- Success will not be in the hands of the *learned*. The winners will be those who are constantly *learning*.
- Continuous education, continuous commitment to learning and an obsession with continuous improvement are vital if one hungers to achieve success.
- Progress does *not* come through a more-of-the-same attitude.
- Rules come and go.
- Somebody has to be better than everybody else.
- It seems to me that the dying words, the very last words, mind you, of each corporate leader who went down with a sinking company ship were likely, "This is *not* the way we've always done it!"
- Challenging conventional wisdom through ideas, information, alternative viewpoints and historical perspective is vital for growth.
- The mind is like a parachute. It only works when it's open.

◇

MYTH ONE

IT WON'T HAPPEN HERE

In 64 AD, Roman Emperor Nero (known as "Caesar") paid little attention to his official duties. Although he viewed himself as both a civic and cultural leader, he spent more time composing music, singing and playing his beloved lyre (a stringed instrument resembling today's violin or fiddle) than governing and leading his empire. Historians debate how and why a great fire broke out in Rome during his reign. Some believed it was set by rebels protesting Nero's lack of civic responsibility; others believed it was simply a natural disaster and still others, including Nero, blamed the fire on Rome's minority Christian community.

Nonetheless, as frantic reports came to Nero that Rome was in flames, he ignored each communiqué and sent each messenger away, no doubt saying something such as, "Rome, in flames? No way. Our aqueduct water system would douse fire quickly. It won't, it can't happen here!"

But it did happen "there." Flames raged for nearly ten days, and most of the city's fourteen regions were destroyed. Legend says that a disbelieving Nero amused himself by playing his musical instrument while thousands died in a city reduced to ashes. Hence, today, if a person ignores his duty, especially in a crisis, we say "...he fiddles while Rome burns!"

Thank goodness that seventeen hundred and eleven years later, most of the colonial townspeople from Cambridge to Lexington, "...through every Middlesex village and farm,"[4] believed Paul Revere when he rode through their rural towns yelling, "The British are coming! The British are coming!" If not, today we might be drinking tea and eating crumpets as opposed to coffee, bagels and cinnamon rolls. Who knows? We could also be saluting the Union Jack instead of Old Glory.

But thankfully, most of the American colonialists living along the route of Revere's ride did heed the warning. History does sadly recall, however, the many New Englanders who ignored the warning and failed to believe patriot Paul's call to arms. Unfortunately, they were the casualties of war. Paraphrasing what they likely said as Revere's hard-working steed galloped past their homes, "Thanks anyway for the warning, Paul, but it won't happen here. It just won't happen here!"

In 1940, all kinds of military intelligence reports and white papers indicated that the U.S. naval base located at Pearl Harbor in Hawaii was vulnerable to Japanese air attack. Washington ignored the reports—even fewer than ten hours before the infamous "sneak attack" warnings of what seemed to be an impending Japanese air raid on Hawaii came into the Pentagon, as well as to both headquarters of the Pacific Fleet and the White House.

Nobody listened. Nobody believed it could happen.

Then, at approximately 4 a.m. on December 7, 1941, the Japanese air force executed their devastatingly sudden air attack on Pearl Harbor and a shocked, disbelieving (i.e., "It won't happen here!") United States plunged into World War II.

"It won't happen here!" Now that's a major myth....

In the late 1960s, Howard Johnson's Restaurants had nearly 1,000 units. They set the standard for success and represented the model for any restaurateur interested in developing a multi-unit operation. Willard Marriott (Hot Shoppes, Marriott Hotels, etc.), Ray Kroc (McDonald's) and other young foodservice entrepreneurs in the '60s envied the Ho Jo model. They wanted their operations to be as good as Howard Johnson's. Ah, if only they knew then what they learned later....

Howard Johnson's was the leader—clear and simple.

They were innovative. Before anyone thought about developing so-called signature products, such as Big Mac, Whopper, etc., Howard Johnson's had the Ho Jo Cola and a complete line of private label candies, syrups and ice creams. They placed units in nontraditional locations (today called alternative channels of distribution) such as on the New Jersey Turnpike, in train stations and in airports. They set up retail shops in the entranceways of their restaurants and sold Ho Jo-branded consumer products. They packaged products for sale in supermarkets, extending their brand reach. They were innovators.

They also were cocky. Howard Johnson's was absolutely convinced they were invincible and that their success would last forever.

Their attitude is best defined by the painful cry, "It won't happen here!"

Well, surprise, surprise. It did happen "here" at Ho Jo.

By the late 1970s, Howard Johnson's started sliding—big time. At their development peak, they had nearly 1,000 restaurants. However, in 1997, with the exception of a few hundred Howard Johnson's hotels, only fifty-three restaurants remained from the fifty-year-old dynasty (perhaps dinosaur is a more relevant word).

Why did they fail?

Here's a list of what went wrong:

- Mismanagement and mismarketing
- No clear vision, mission or positioning
- Inexperienced, incapable leadership
- Poor advice and direction on resource allocation
- Irrelevant menu that refused to change with the times
- Slow service levels and antiquated service systems
- Failure to adapt and adjust to consumer "need states"

Perhaps the most important reason for their demise, however, is that they honestly, blindly refused to accept the fact that "the unbeatable" can be beaten...that the "can't miss" surely can miss and that nothing is forever. They fell prey to the "It won't happen here!" monster.

In 1980, Eastern Air Lines was the second-largest carrier in the world. They were dynamic, successful and profitable. In fact, at the height of their success, in the early 1980s, Eastern's revenues exceeded $4 billion. They were viewed as innovators when they introduced the Boeing 727. They were highly respected and valued by business travelers for the development of their shuttle, which provided hourly airplane service among the cities of New York, Boston, Philadelphia and Washington D.C.

During its heyday, former astronaut Frank Borman was Eastern Air Lines' celebrated leader. Business was great and, in all likelihood, the phrase, "It won't happen here!" echoed throughout the halls of Eastern's lavish Miami headquarters.

But things changed. Things shifted. In 1986, after a "hostile takeover" by Frank Lorenzo and Texas Air, the shift hit the fan (or in this case, the propeller).

Poor route structures, bad acquisitions, a huge debt partly created by a landmark labor dispute, management vanity and arrogance, key executive resignations, years of bitter union strikes, allegations of "asset stripping" and multibillion dollar losses all contributed to Eastern's demise.

On Saturday, January 19, 1991, Eastern Air Lines, Inc. ceased operating. More than 20,000 employees lost their jobs, about 200 jets and turboprop airplanes were grounded and there was less than $115 million left in Eastern's bank account to pay more than $1 billion in unsecured creditors' claims. Each creditor received, on average, less than one-cent for each dollar Eastern owed them.

What happened?

Hey, what ever happened to the power of brands like Ovaltine? Bosco? Metrical? Sambo's Restaurants? Lucky Strike? Postum? The Henry-J automobile? National Airlines? Sen-Sen? Studebaker?

―――― ◇ ――――

Industries, companies, traditions, lifestyles and
careers that fail to adapt and adjust to change die.
It's simple. It's brutal. It's reality.

―――― ◇ ――――

"It won't happen here!" That's what I call a water sandwich! When will we start learning from history? Too many people buy smoke detectors after a fire. That's poor timing. I remember reading somewhere that it's probably important to remember that Noah started building his ark before it started raining. That's better timing.

W.T. Grant was the largest discount department store chain in the United States in 1972, with 1,208 stores. In fact, when Sam Walton was operating his very first store, a Ben Franklin "Five n' Dime," in rural Arkansas, W.T. Grant was America's most successful retailer. Walton envied W.T. Grant and often spoke of how he would, one day, like to see his business operate as efficiently and successfully as the New York-based giant.

Of course, Walton observed W.T. Grant from afar and didn't see the blemishes and the flaws. As he got closer to their business and probed for more information, he realized that Grant proved to serve as a better lesson on how *not* to conduct business.

For instance, W.T. Grant marketed their own private label brands to excess and avoided relationships with national power brands. In fact, more than seventy percent of the merchandise they displayed had the W.T. Grant name on it.

They also confused the public. Their positioning was unclear and confusing. Were they a variety chain? A discounter? A department store? A hard goods merchant? Their marketing programs were all across the board. When asked, most consumers couldn't define the Grant concept.

W.T. Grant also overextended themselves financially. They tried to expand much too quickly without the controls and resources that rapid growth requires. They were also highly leveraged as well as very undercapitalized.

As if this weren't enough, inadequate, ineffectual leadership led to an incredibly high rate of employee turnover, especially at the management level. Surviving and remaining management team members didn't have the experience, depth or the capabilities to fulfill the company's aggressive growth objectives and, eventually, morale declined.

The final bombshell hit in the early 1970s when W.T. Grant launched a major media and public relations campaign touting its innovative consumer credit program. Although the program turned out to move a great deal of product from retail shelves, it also led to disastrous uncollectable accounts and credit writeoffs. Eventually, these killed the retail giant.

Throughout their run, they, too, must have said, "It won't happen here!"

But it did happen to W.T. Grant.

On November 2, 1975, W.T. Grant filed for bankruptcy. One thousand seventy-three stores were closed and 80,000 people were put out of work. Their creditors had to write off approximately $234 million in bad loans and their suppliers ended up with $110 million in unpaid loans.

And yet, they were *numero uno* in mass retailing. Today, only old guys like me remember them.

——— ◇ ———

The first one now might later be last...

——— ◇ ———

History is full of dinosaurs that couldn't adapt and adjust. The brontosaurus went from distinction to extinction. Gone, also, are industries and companies that couldn't change with the times and that refused to accept the fact that everyone is a possible target for disaster. ("It won't happen here.")

In 1972 and again in 1982, IBM was the No. 1 company in the world by stock market valuation, with market values of $46.8 billion and $57.0 billion, respectively. By 1992, not only had they lost their No. 1 position, but they had fallen to twenty-sixth at year-end with a huge drop in market value to $29 billion.

That's quite an achievement, no?

After losing an incredible $28 billion in market value in just ten short years, it's hard to imagine that any "Big Blue" executive would ever again walk the halls of IBM headquarters saying, "It won't happen here!"

The irony is that IBM Chairman Thomas J. Watson, Jr., (1956-1971) told an audience at Columbia University "...corporations are expendable and success...at best...is an impermanent achievement which can always slip out of hand."

Obviously, the key executives at IBM didn't listen to or accept Watson's wisdom. In 1992, success slipped "out of hand."

Further irony is that Watson's predecessor, his father, Thomas J. Watson, Sr., IBM's founder, said many years earlier, "It is harder to keep a business great than it is to build it."

Somebody should have listened to the Watsons!

History books are filled with stories of company executives who deceived themselves into believing their companies were invincible and their career success was forever.

From the years 1992-1994, there were lots of resumes out "on the street" carrying the names of former Sears executives who once actually believed their success was forever. Each waved the "It won't happen here!" banner proudly and refused to acknowledge, much less recognize, the tremendous challenges coming from a wide range of formidable competitors—especially Kmart and Wal-Mart.[5] And so, in 1992, although Sears had once been retailing's innovator and leader, they posted losses of $3.9 billion. Their total sales were about $32 billion, while Kmart's sales were $39 billion (with gross profits of approximately $940 million) and Wal-Mart's sales were in excess of $55 billion (with a gross profit of approximately $2 billion).

Sam Walton, in his autobiography, *Sam Walton: Made In America* (written with John Huey), wrote, "One reason Sears fell so far off the pace is that they wouldn't admit for the longest time that Wal-Mart and Kmart were their real competition. They ignored both of us, and we both blew right by them."

"It won't happen here." Myth, myth!

Aren't we here forever?

As stated in this book's introduction: Change is inevitable. Growth is optional.

———— ◇ ————

Again, the one constant in life is that things change.
But change is surely not new.
What's new is the incredible speed of change.

———— ◇ ————

The very nature of change has changed. The pace of change is out of control and barely predictable. It absolutely ain't what it used to be!

To reiterate a vital point, when confronted with change—fast-paced change—one only has three choices, namely:

1. Ignore it.
2. React to it.
3. Make other changes.

Ignoring it is a sure way to go from distinction to extinction. ("It won't...it can't happen here.")

Reacting, adapting and adjusting to change is certainly important for survival. If you want to thrive (as opposed to merely survive) and experience quantum leap achievement, make other changes.

Yes, change agents, change masters, change catalysts, change inventors and innovators of change construct their own future.

Through an ongoing process of reinvention and redefinition, they ensure themselves of a future so that "It truly won't happen here."

Throughout the history of time, the *unsinkable sunk* (i.e., the Titanic); *the indestructible was destroyed* (i.e., The Holy Roman Empire); *the unbeatable was beaten* (i.e., Nazi Germany and Japan in World War II); *the uncontrollable was controlled* (i.e., Niagara Falls); *the incredible became credible* (i.e., astronauts walked on the moon, bioengineers created life in a test tube); *the unbelievable became believable* (i.e., a human heart was transplanted); and *the unthinkable became thinkable* (i.e., scientists cloned a sheep).

THE "CAN'T MISS" CAN MISS

Blockbuster Video, IBM, Boston Market, McDonalds, Ben & Jerry's, Kupehenheimer Men's Stores, 7-11, even Kmart, all couldn't miss. Yet, they all missed. They faltered. They all went through some very tough times.

Some recovered. Some haven't.

For example, Blockbuster sales went incredibly flat in 1997 after huge volume growth in the early 1990s. In fact, after Blockbuster was purchased by Viacom in 1994 for $8 billion, its pre-merger cash flow projections have fallen short by $200 million. IBM lost more than $5 billion in 1992. Boston Market grew to more than 800 units in 1996, but fell so flat in sales and grossly underperformed, their stock decreased from approximately $40 a share to less than $6 a share in the Spring of 1997.

Some say problems come in threes. "Can't miss" McDonalds proved that when they faltered with their Health Express dinner house concept. Then the ineffectual McLean "better-for-you product" failed to take off and, finally, their disastrous 55-cent hamburger promotion failed (which also led to a number of key executives finding their careers in jeopardy as a result of the debacle).

Kmart nearly went down for the count, closing stores, enduring huge sales deficits, losing share to its competitors and mismanaging like crazy in the mid-1990s. For this, it earned the questionable distinction of making it to *Fortune* Magazine's "Least Admired Companies" list in 1994, 1995, 1996 and 1997. That's quite a streak!

I wish I had the "It won't happen here!" banner franchise. I would have made a fortune selling signs to executives at these "can't miss" companies.

In 1996, I discovered a neat little gadget produced by Panasonic. Called a "Business Card Reader," this electronic file has the capability of scanning business cards and storing pertinent information from each card (i.e., name, title, company, address, phone, fax, etc.) in a well-organized, cross-referenced electronic file. It's small, fits in your hand and stores about 500 business cards. Wow, I thought! What a neat idea. I'll take two!

As if it were fate, I was flying on a Delta Airlines jet a few days after purchasing this wonderful gadget and struck up a conversation with a gentleman sitting next to me. When I learned that he was, coincidentally, a regional vice-president for Rolodex, the historical leader in business card cataloguing, I excitedly showed him my new Panasonic electronic business card caddy and asked him what he thought of it.

He was smug. He was cocky. He sloughed off the Panasonic gadget as a gimmick, as a fad, as a piece of junk that would never pass the test of time. After all, he said, "Nobody will ever surpass Rolodex for cataloguing business cards. That's our business. We're the leaders. Panasonic should stick to producing musical sound systems and televisions." Although he didn't say the words, per se, I must admit he had that obnoxious look about him that seemed ready to say, "It won't happen here!"

Now the way I figured it, he probably should be looking for a new job soon. After all, Rolodex, with its traditional rotary wheel of business cards is paper driven. It's cumbersome. It certainly doesn't fit in one's hand nor does it travel well. It's made to sit in a prominent place on one's desk.

On the other hand, my portable Panasonic card file is electronic, paperless and very convenient. It fits nicely in my hand and hardly takes up any space in my briefcase. I can even download stored information onto my computer. Yes, one day, if Rolodex doesn't respond to this Panasonic shot-across-the-bow, we'll likely be saying to our associates, "I know I have Frank's phone number. Let me quickly pull it up on my Panasonic" (as opposed to looking up a number on one's "Rolodex").

Why do so many lack vision? Nothing, absolutely nothing, is forever. Consider these wonderful, myopic, visionless quotations.

———— ◇ ————

Everything that can be invented has been invented.
—Charles H. Duell, Director of the U.S. Patent Office, 1899

———— ◇ ————

Heavier-than-air flying machines are impossible.
Man will never fly!
—Lord Kelvin, President, Royal Society, 1895

———— ◇ ————

Sensible and responsible women do not want to vote.
—Grover Cleveland, President of the United States

———— ◇ ————

There is no likelihood man can ever tap the power of the atom.
—Robert Millikan, Nobel Prize in Physics, 1923

———— ◇ ————

Who the hell wants to hear actors talk?
—Harry M. Warner, Chairman, Warner Brothers Pictures, 1927

———— ◇ ————

Nothing is forever. Fail to adapt and adjust to change and you die a painful death. Close your mind to new ideas and new possibilities and you're on a course set for disaster.

———— ◇ ————

After all, there's only one rule in our world and that one rule, simply and succinctly, is "There are no rules!"

———— ◇ ————

Too often, business people become paralyzed by their paradigms. "Paradigm"—now that's a much-maligned, overused business word.

What's a "paradigm?"

A paradigm is a model, a standard. Paradigms shift. And as paradigms shift, we, too, need to adapt and adjust. We need to embrace change.

Again, it's not that change is new. It's the speed of change that's new. Blink your eyes and there's a whole new world before you, a whole new ballgame.

For instance, we had some reception problems with a secondary television set located in our home basement playroom. I took the set to a TV repair shop and told the storekeeper about our problems. I then said something stupid—something really very stupid.

I said to the repairman, "Look, once you've fixed the set perhaps it makes sense for you to check the tubes, you know, clean 'em up a little bit, make sure they're good."

He looked at me as if I just landed on Earth from another planet.

"Tubes?" he asked. "Are you serious? There aren't any tubes, plural, in this set. There's only one tube—the TV tube. Multiple tubes in television sets went out in 1980. Where have you been?"

Yes, where have I been?

I felt like an idiot, yet, thinking back, I'm not sure I've had any problems with any television set I've owned since the early 1980s. I just figured there still were those little replaceable tubes in the set. You know, the ones we could buy at the local supermarket or drug store and fix ourselves.

———— ◇ ————

Well, when you're through learning, you're through.

———— ◇ ————

Change happens....constantly, constantly.

We're now moving faster than the speed of life. We've become a society that even pays to project itself into "virtual reality." In fact, John Deere, the mammoth heavy equipment company, introduced a "virtual tractor" powered by a CD-ROM so that prospective customers can "test drive" farm equipment right in a John Deere store showroom. Personally, I'd be concerned I would fall off the tractor and sustain a virtual injury.

Desktop publishing is pervasive. Soon we'll have "desktop manufacturing." Things are happening fast!

What's on the horizon? How about "just in time" education or even "virtual education?" Education is "in" but school, as we knew it, will likely be "out."

Impossible? You say you don't believe it? Just remember that wonderful Mark Twain quote, "For man, all things are possible 'cept to have a hole in his pants and keep his fingers out of it!"

Yes, it can happen here, wherever your "here" happens to be. If we're not poised and ready for change—and if we don't embrace change, it will overtake us.

———— ◇ ————

Change has no conscience. It affects companies
large and small.

———— ◇ ————

Change also affects our lives and our lifestyles. What ever happened to rotary telephones, elevator operators, girdles, bomb shelters, doctors making house calls, enclosed telephone booths, reel-to-reel tape recorders, full-service gasoline pump attendants, soda fountains that made cola drinks from real Coke syrup and a myriad of other products and tidbits of culture now just memories and nostalgia. Late in 1997, for example, I saw an IBM Electric Typewriter with flowers displayed in it being merchandised for sale in an antique shop window. Wow!

Our world is exploding with changes, faster than ever before.

Don't believe anyone who tries to convince you that "It won't happen here!"

The Boy Scouts of America have always had the right idea. "Be prepared!" is their motto.

We live in a world of surprises. Be prepared!

Challenge the Myths of
Your Own Conventional Wisdom...

CHAPTER HIGHLIGHTS

- Nothing is forever!
- Industries, companies, traditions, lifestyles and careers that fail to adapt and adjust to change die. It's simple. It's brutal. It's reality.
- History is full of dinosaurs that couldn't adapt and adjust. The brontosaurus went from distinction to extinction and is gone—so are many industries, companies and even careers.

- Too many company executives who became casualties deceived themselves into believing their companies were invincible and their career successes were forever.
- Throughout the history of time, the unsinkable sank, the indestructible was destroyed, the unbeatable was beaten, the uncontrollable was controlled, the incredible became credible, the unbelievable turned believable and the unthinkable became thinkable.
- The "can't miss" *can* miss.
- There's only one rule in our world and that one rule, simply and succinctly, is "There are no rules!"
- When you're through learning, you are through!
- Change has no conscience. It affects companies big and small.
- We live in a world of surprises. Be prepared!

◇

MYTH TWO

THE FUTURE IS OUT OF OUR CONTROL

"Que sera, sera,"[6] is a refrain from an old 1950s song that means "Whatever will be, will be." The assumption is that the future is out of our conrol and not for us to envision.

I disagree.

The future, in fact, *is* ours to see and is absolutely *not* out of our control.

The legendary management guru, Peter Drucker, summed it up best when he told a disciple, "It you want to predict the future, create it!"

Create the future? Now, that's a novel idea. No, that's a wonderful, proactive, great idea.

Why wait?

The key to creating the future is to understand the logical and likely direction the world is traveling, then to simply speed up the process. What will consumers be like? What will the economy be like? What kinds of technology are on the horizon? What are the likely trends and developments in manufacturing, packaging, distribution, logistics, operations, finance, material handling, marketing, sales, human resources and other disciplines, as well as other functional areas?

Where is it all going?

Once you have a sense of direction, it's time to develop strategies, tactics, guiding principles, products, programs and services to match your future view. *That's* creating the future.

We're forever subscribing to, reading about and learning of forecasts and predictions for the future presented by the current hot visionaries, soothsayers and futurists. The key isn't their forecasts. What's vital is the application, utilization and employment of each prognostication.

Peter Drucker, in addition to being a professor, author and lecturer, has served as a trusted adviser to many leading companies and counseled many corporate executives. In my early years as a consultant to the Coca-Cola Company, I remember hearing a story about how Coke's former president, Don Keough, would spend a day with Drucker every so often just to learn from the master and gain insight on various business strategies, ideas, thinking, etc.

As the story goes, at the end of a particularly fruitful day, Keough turned to the professor and told him how very much he had learned and how inspired he was as a result of their time together. Drucker, in turn, replied something to the effect of, "Don't tell me how much you've learned today. Tell me what you're going to do with the learning tomorrow morning at 9 a.m."

Tomorrow at 9 a.m. There it is. Bingo!

The key to success is *not* the information, the knowledge, the ideas, the data, the education or the prediction—it's the application. In other words, once there's a pretty good idea of what's on the horizon for an industry, business, category, product, career, etc., what will happen tomorrow at 9 a.m? The threshold question, then, is, *If this forecast of ours for the future is real, accurate and likely to become a reality, what are we doing TODAY to prepare for TOMORROW?*

National Hockey League superstar Wayne Gretzky said it best when asked what he thought was the key to his incredibly successful pro hockey career. Gretzky replied:

"I guess it all has to do with the puck. You see, most other players watch where the puck is. My focus is always directed at where the puck is going."

If we had focused our attention, applied our resources and directed all efforts at "where the puck (business, consumer, economy, etc.) was going," then we'd surely be poised and ready to create a hot, meaningful future. On the other hand, if we focus energy on "where the puck is" (the current state of business affairs), then we'd likely be left out in the cold with a business that was frozen in time and stagnant.

Throughout history, soothsayers and visionaries have forecast future trends by focusing on the same basic seven categories. They are:

- Population
- Demographics
- Education
- Technology
- Food
- Energy
- Communications

By logically deducing the direction, for example, of consumer demographics or technology, especially as related to your industry and business, dynamic plans to "create the future" can be designed and developed.

Success-oriented business people should commit resources to create, develop, execute and manage innovative new programs, processes and products that match these very important areas.

For instance, what are you and your company doing about the fact that the global economy is growing at approximately 4.5 percent per year?

———— ◇ ————

Isn't it time resources are slammed against where the puck is going?

———— ◇ ————

As an aside, note that "technology" is on the above list. I heard a wonderful forecast regarding technology, attributed to Professor Warren Bennis of the University of Southern California, who humorously noted, "The factory of the future will have two employees, a man and a dog. The man will be there to feed the dog and the dog will be there to bite the man if he dare touch any of the equipment."

—— ◇ ——

The big question, again, obviously is,
"What are we doing about the logical, likely future?"

—— ◇ ——

For whatever reason, many people think that when a discussion of the future comes up, it must be geared toward five, even ten years out. But the future is tomorrow, next week, next month, next quarter, next year. How far out one plans is directly related to specific, individual corporate (and career) needs. Winston Churchill said, "It is a mistake to look too far ahead. Only one link in the chain of destiny can be handled at a time."

On another note, I am also convinced that if we anticipate and envision a future wrought with pain, suffering, problems and failures, our greatest fears will be realized. Attitude oftentimes dictates, defines and directs future occurrences.

Think positively and good things will follow. Think negatively and watch the future unfurl with doom and gloom. If you convince yourself that the future is dark and dreary, it will become so. Some call this the *self-fulfilling prophesy*. Positivism is a key ingredient for creating a promising future.

Logically, we can predict the future. Once we predict it, we can prepare for it and capitalize on its direction.

H.G. Wells accurately forecast specific modes of space travel as well as travel below the sea through a well-organized system of logical deductions. From biodome cities to submarines, Wells envisioned a high-tech future filled with efficient, high-speed travel. NASA archives show that modern scientists have used many of H.G. Wells' ideas, postulates and models in their space development programs.

Author (and futurist) George Orwell[7] may have been off by a dozen or so years in the forecasts he presented in his book *1984* (published in 1949). Nonetheless, he was incredibly "spot on" with his prognostications. For instance, his prediction that we would be obsessively focused on a television-like screen called "Big Brother," which could dramatically influence, if not control, our lives certainly has some basis in reality today. Instead of "Big Brother," my family calls the screen "television," "computer," "boob tube," "Nintendo," "Sega," "Playstation" and "Cable." Regardless of the moniker, the screen is real and important, and holds a central place in millions of homes around the world. And it does influence, if not control, many lives and behavior patterns.

Whether the future is bright or bleak is all in the mind (and mindset) of the beholder.

H.G. Wells saw a positive future with incredible technological advances. George Orwell, on the other hand, offered predictions that were dismal, dreary, disheartening and grim. Wells lived a prosperous, happy, fulfilled life, while Orwell's life met with a lonely, tragic and painful death (the *self-fulfilling prophesy* at work, perhaps).

Wells once said, "Thoughts of tomorrow are wonderful, exciting and brilliant. Bring on the advances. Bring on the speed. I can hardly wait." There's energy in his words. There's optimism in his tone.

Orwell once said, "If you want a picture of the future, imagine a boot stomping on a human face...forever!"

Happy guy, no? My advice is to not even entertain thoughts of a bleak future. Don't go there! Think only about the brightest of bright futures. The creation of a fertile, fruitful, flourishing future begins with a positive state of mind. Period! When forecasting and, ultimately, creating the future, yesterday and today can serve as very important tools to define and create a positive tomorrow.

The past provides the foundation for planning for the future. Once you've asked yourself the following questions, which are designed to help you review your business past, you'll be well on your way to shaping the future.

Using my own consulting company, CO-OPPORTUNITIES, Inc. as a real example for you to review, the following items represent the threshold questions I believe you, too, must answer.

WHERE DID WE START?

CO-OPPORTUNITIES, Inc. began in 1990 at a time when many American companies were downsizing and seeking outsourced ideas, information, assistance and counsel from "subject matter experts."

WHY DID WE START?

CO-OPPORTUNITIES, Inc. realized that many traditional ways of doing business were no longer relevant. Therefore, we decided to provide clients with strategic counsel and direction that was out-of-the-box in its nontraditional approach to challenging conventional wisdom.

HOW DID WE START?

We realized that Coca-Cola was fighting a huge share war against Pepsi-Cola on an uneven battlefield. Coke was strictly a "beverage company." Pepsi, at the time, was a "food company" by virtue of their ownership of Pizza Hut, Taco Bell, Kentucky Fried Chicken, FritoLay, etc. Therefore, we built a long-term consulting relationship with Coca-Cola to help them level the playing field.

WHAT WAS OUR INITIAL VISION?

CO-OPPORTUNITIES, Inc. was to be a leading consulting firm that focused its activities on providing out-of-the-box solutions for world-class clients, assisting them in creating nontraditional approaches to business development.

WHAT WAS OUR COMPANY MISSION?

CO-OPPORTUNITIES, Inc. strives to be a leading counselor to multinational clients, assisting them in creating, developing and effectively implementing nontraditional strategies geared toward business development and quantum leap growth.

WHAT WERE OUR ORIGINAL "GUIDING PRINCIPLES?"

Here are a few examples of our guiding principles:

1. To maintain a manageable number of multinational, world class clients on long-term retainer contracts, as opposed to the more traditional consulting practice based on project-by-project positioning.
2. To develop our primary client relationships (and reporting channels) to/through the top officers of client companies (i.e., chairman, CEO, etc.)

WHAT CUSTOMER OR CONSUMER NEEDS DID WE FILL?

Every company and every client needs someone to "question answers" as well as to "answer questions." Our role was to constantly ask the question "Why?" and to serve as the contrarian voice in the business-building process. Ever challenging conventional wisdom, we led our clients toward questioning everything and looking at their world differently.

WHAT WORKED FOR US? WHAT DIDN'T WORK FOR US?

Two examples for your review.

1. What *Did Not* Work:

    We initially accepted clients of all sizes, scopes, and in a wide range of development stages. This proved to be complex and we found ourselves being less effective than when we worked with/for clients that were multinational, mature and well-established.

2. What *Did* Work:

    We found an important niche and a discernible point of unique difference when we started facilitating strategic alliances for our clients (with similar and dissimilar companies—even with competitive companies). Every alliance or joint venture requires a middleman to fairly and equitably construct and, often, to manage the venture.

WHAT WAS THE LONG-TERM VISION FOR THE BUSINESS?

Simply put, our long-term vision for CO-OPPORTUNITIES, Inc. was to become a *leader* in the niche in which we operated and focused, as well as to make an important difference for our clients. Targeted objectives were to be perceived as a "nonpaid member of our client's team" and an "extension of their business."

Once we do a self-analysis and review "where we are" versus "where we plan to be" in the development of our company, we can make adjustments, focus on continuous improvement and set new (or renewed) objectives for our company. That will help us craft our business future.

Where we are likely to be going or *where we need to be going* usually is best understood when viewing a template that defines *where we've been* and *where we currently are.* It's almost algebraic. A (Past) + B (Present) = C (Logical Future).

Is this exact? No! Does it come close. Yes! All we can hope for is to come close with our forecasts. Once again, however, don't forget that the *big idea* is to "create *the* future." If you keep that in mind, you'll *always* be exactly on target with your forecast. You'll always be right!

It's a trite expression but there truly is a future for those who plan for it. Trite but true. No matter how discontinuous our miniaturized, digitized, synthesized, deregulated world may seem to be, planning will make sense out of it all.

Planning is vital in preparing for the logical, likely future. It is critical for those courageous business people who chart new courses and create new industries, enterprises, products, programs, services, etc.

Len Chandler, a 1960s poet and folk singer, wrote about two sailing ships traveling in different directions, even though they both were confronted by the very same ocean breeze. He logically concluded it was "the set of the sail, not the gale"[8] that defined their course.

Absolutely. Right on! We all are equally confronted and challenged by the same winds of change. It is how each of us set our own business (and career) sails that "bids" each of us "where to go" and to what specific port we ultimately dock.

The wonderfully similar thing about both managing a business and steering a vessel on the high seas is that if you should encounter stormy, threatening conditions, charting a new course can quickly calm down and neutralize even the most ominous situation. Never forget that if you are bold enough to create the future, you can also become bolder and revise, reposition, reinvigorate and recreate that very same future when necessary. Just as we possess the power to set, as well as reset, our sails, we also control the tempo of our lives and businesses.

Sam Walton, always a terrific case study to review, was a man who not only controlled the tempo of his life, but also harnessed the energy of his employees (called associates), suppliers (called partners) and investors to build a retailing system totally focused on customer service. With an energetic mindset oriented toward innovative mass merchandising, he invented a culture designed to create an improved model for the future of the entire retailing industry.

In 1945, when Sam Walton was the owner-manager of a small Ben Franklin five-and-dime in Newport, Arkansas, he was dissatisfied with the state of general merchandise store retailing and decided to start his own enterprise. He developed a vision and a comprehensive plan for reinventing the discount store business.

His new chain, Wal-Mart, would not be limited to the traditional on-shelf offerings found in what he called the "me, too" general merchandise stores. Wal-Mart expanded its line of consumer goods to an unbelievable level of product offerings (called stock keeping units or SKUs) with a range of products and services never before merchandised under one retail roof.

Disagreeing with the then current standard industry practice of marketing second-tier branded products at reduced prices and leading brands at premium prices, Sam Walton worked diligently to craft the most powerful and effective retail purchasing machine in the United States. This purchasing powerhouse leveraged the equities of big brands, while leveling their big brand egos in the process, to create what would become the future of mass merchandising embodied in the phrase, "national brands at everyday low prices" (now affectionately called "EDLP" by all types of retailers.

He also established the foundation for a unique supplier-partner system that had never before existed in retailing. Walton required his key supplier-partners to set up Wal-Mart specific offices near Bentonville, Arkansas, the home of its corporate office. These "dedicated" field offices and their resident supplier personnel had one—and only one—responsibility: to effectively and efficiently serve and service Wal-Mart! Procter and Gamble (P&G) is one example of a number of key Wal-Mart suppliers that established Wal-Mart dedicated offices adjacent to the chain's headquarters. Many key Wal-Mart supplier-employees today still carry business cards that have both their company logo and the Wal-Mart logo embossed on the card, boldly declaring their focused support of mighty customer Wal-Mart.

Walton developed a culture oriented toward creating the future every day and every year. He added pharmacies, optical shops, in-store bakeries, food service departments with real fast-food brands (i.e., McDonald's), floral departments, home decorating centers, hair stylist shops and more—all to provide customers a comprehensive merchandising mix.

He also created one of the most powerful private label brands in history, "Sam's Choice." He viewed his stores as laboratories and tested constantly. He reinvented and refined the warehouse club store concept with his successful Sam's Club. He developed a city-like mega-store called the Hypermart (more than 250,000 square feet of retail sales space) and he also bundled a supermarket concept with a traditional Wal-Mart, creating a chain of "combo stores" known as Wal*Mart Super Centers.[9] These Super Centers have been incredibly successful and have given many a traditional supermarket operator stress and lots of headaches.

After his death, his associates continued inventing, creating and re-creating retailing with the same spirit, energy and vigor characteristic of their visionary leader.

Sam set the stage. In reality, Sam invented the stage. He created retailing's future.

This all sounds easy, but it wasn't. Some of his early retailing strategies bombed. Walton fell flat on his face a number of times before succeeding.

Speaking of "flat," Walt Disney had so many disastrous creative failures that at one point he was "flat broke" and had to borrow money at near-usurious rates to avoid bankruptcy. In fact, in 1939, in order to continue funding his effort to create the future of animation and entertainment, he was forced to take his company public just to gain working cash flow.

Hotel magnate Conrad Hilton also endured some very tough times in his early entrepreneurial days. He lost a great deal of money and was almost forced to close his first hotel before eventually finding the right formula for lodging success.

Sam Walton, Walt Disney, Conrad Hilton and a very long list of other innovators and successful business people all struggled in their early days, their hungry years. Each failed a number of times. Through it all, however, they kept their dreams alive and their visions of the future clear. They persevered, worked very hard and ultimately succeeded by inventing a new direction for each of their respective industries and enterprises.

It takes vision to see where an industry or a business is going. It takes "guts" to take that vision and invent a program that is actionable, viable and that fits the vision. It also takes hard work, lots of sweat equity, dedication and a near-obsessive commitment to excellence to bring it all together and to succeed.

Thomas Edison said, "To succeed, one needs to blend aspiration, inspiration and perspiration." Ironically enough, Sam Walton, Walt Disney and Conrad Hilton all claimed to be "overnight successes"— in about twenty-five years.

Hey, it's simple. No guts. No glory!

It's important to note that Walton, Disney, Hilton and a host of other innovators who have successfully created new industries and businesses, all committed resources toward planning.

There's a future for those who plan for it.

Hurricanes happen. Tornadoes happen. Sunshine and rain showers happen. But successfully creating the future doesn't just happen: It requires a plan.

Planning for the future has to be realistic, relevant, logical and actionable. No pie-in-the-sky here. If all one does is slam resources against the planning process and produce pages upon pages of "stuff" (technical term for "things") that have no basis in reality and are incapable of being converted into "kick'em in the pants" action...it will all be for naught.

Scratch it out on a napkin after a few Michelob Lights. Write its key elements on a self-sticking note while you're commuting in traffic. Plug ideas into your computer after hours while watching a TV sitcom. It matters not how you plan, where you plan, the way you plan or what the plan looks like in the end.

The key is to plan.

As long as the final product is bulletproof, seamless, well-thought-out, relevant to your specific enterprise and *actionable*, it will provide you a road map to the future.

I always take great delight in sharing my favorite plan example with friends, clients, associates, audiences and now, readers.

When my son Eric was ten-years-old, he came to me and asked if I would buy him a compact disc player.

Seizing his inquiry as a teaching opportunity, I told him, "Eric, let's make a deal. You find out how much the CD player costs and if you earn half its price, I'll give you the other half. In the banking world, they call that 'matching funds.' Now what I'd suggest you do is run up to your room, sit down at your desk and write out a business plan—you know, ways that you can make some money." Eric was the kind of child who always enjoyed a challenge and so he wrote a "business plan." I'm thrilled to share it with you:

WAYS TO MAKE MONEY
1. Shuvel Snow
2. Work In the Yard
3. Bet On Football Games
4. Chores
5. Find It On The Ground

"Shovel snow" may seem like a great idea, except that we live in Atlanta. It snows here religiously once every four years. Not a big idea, not a big revenue opportunity.

"Work in the yard." That's cool. That's a strategy. However, I'm still trying to figure out how he and our paid gardener are going to divvy up the duties (and split the fee).

"Bet on football games." That strategy got me in a lot of trouble with my wife, Kim, who, concerned, asked, "What are you teaching the children?" Thinking about this specific strategy further, however, I must admit that betting against the Atlanta Falcons is probably a sure way for Eric to make some money.

"Do chores." That works. That's a strategy.

"Find it on the ground!" Now, that's the best. An interesting strategy, no? You see, Eric's younger brother, Jeffrey, and I went shopping. Jeffrey found $7 on the floor by the cashier's checkout station. Pretty lucky! Eric thought about Jeffrey's "find." He then decided that if he started walking through stores and malls bent over, constantly surveying the floor, he, too, would likely find some cash. Eric was convinced this strategy could make him a rich kid.

The irony is that so many business people are convinced that a bright, successful, rich future is going to be setting on the ground, just waiting to be picked up.

Reader, you're not going to find the keys to a successful future on the ground.

Get serious! All one ever finds on the ground is dirt, gravel, dust and other "things" (technical term for "stuff").

Successfully creating the future can only come through the development and effective execution of a plan.

We can sit back and idly wait for the future to arrive and hope our companies, products and personal core competencies fit. We can pray that we'll survive, that we'll "make the cut." I personally find that proposition pretty scary and very uncertain, don't you?

On the other hand, we can invent the future and create our own destiny through vision, education, energy and planning.

Things are moving fast. Tomorrow is almost upon us.

Yes, there's a future for those who plan for it. Fictional cartoon character Daddy Warbuck's adopted little girl, Annie, sang about tomorrow being "only a day away." Get moving. (It's only a day away.)

Challenge the Myths of Your Own Conventional Wisdom...

CHAPTER HIGHLIGHTS

- The key to creating the future is to understand the logical and likely direction the world is traveling, then to simply speed up the process.
- The real key—after having experienced a day of enthusiastic, energetic, highly spirited, education-filled learning—is what you do with it "tomorrow morning at 9 a.m!"
- Focus your efforts on "where the puck is *going*."
- Success doesn't come from information, knowledge, ideas, data, education or realistic forecasts. It's the application that's the critical ingredient.

- The most important trend categories to consider in planning for the future are:
  - ◇ Population
  - ◇ Demographics
  - ◇ Education
  - ◇ Technology
  - ◇ Food
  - ◇ Energy
  - ◇ Communications
- Creating a fruitful, fertile, flourishing future starts with a positive state of mind.
- There truly is a future for those who plan for it.
  - ◇ It takes vision to see where an industry or business is going.
  - ◇ It takes "guts" to take that vision and invent a program that is actionable, viable and one that fits the vision.
- No guts. No glory!

◇

MYTH THREE

FOLLOW THE LEADER

Robert Frost wrote in his classic poem, "The Road Not Taken,"

> "...two roads diverged in a wood, and I—
> I took the one less traveled by,
> And that has made all the difference." [10]

It's amazing how so many great innovations and successes have come about because companies and leaders made a difference by charting courses on roads "less traveled on."

> After all, most great works of art, industry and
> science came about because someone
> looked at the world differently.

——— ◇ ———

Learn from leaders but ultimately, chart your own unique course and follow your head and your heart instead.

You see, there's an inherent problem with leaders. They are, typically, "one of a kind."

From "Give 'em hell, Harry (Truman)" to John Lennon...from General Dwight David Eisenhower to Astronaut John Glenn...from Coach Vince Lombardi to Thomas Alva Edison...leaders are a unique breed of cat.

This goes for leading companies and products as well.

Each of us, at some time, has said, "There will never be another..."

Actually, there won't be "another!"

And that's okay.

There will, however, be an "other." Yes, other people, companies and products will come along and become leading and leaders. It's the natural course of affairs.

Through it all, however, leadership doesn't just happen. Carefully blending public need, uniqueness, strong competencies and great communication may very well bring forth leadership.

Imitators have tried to follow in Ronald McDonald's footsteps and wrest hamburger share away from the "golden arches" for years. All to no avail. Many companies have tried to follow what they perceived as the Hallmark Cards' culture and "growth imperatives" (world class creativity, an obsession with being the best in its class, delivering morally and spiritually sound messages, etc.). Again, to no avail.

There is only *one* Nordstrom, *one* Crate & Barrel, *one* Nike, *one* Toys 'R' Us, *one* Virgin Atlantic Airways, *one* Motorola, *one* Intel, *one* Mirage Resort, *one* Microsoft, *one* Rubbermaid, *one* Godiva Chocolate...*one, one, one*...I think you get my point.

So, if we play by the rules of logic, it's a "no brainer" to conclude that great success comes forth from innovation—*not* imitation—and that leadership comes from a strong focus on creating, developing, implementing, managing and living the unique.

"Following the leader" is a great kids game but in business, it is a myth that will likely get a company (and career) into trouble.

Why?

Simply put, most people, companies and products absolutely cannot live up to the level of the leader. They just can't measure up to the standards set by a leading executive, company or product.

But in the end, it's not just the standards set by the leader that are important. Successful leaders and leadership are defined more in the eyes of the receiver ("follower") than in the perception of the sender ("leader"). John Gardener, former White House cabinet member and also founder of the national lobbying group, Common Cause, said, "Leadership is won when people believe that the leader is capable of meeting their needs."

It's about perception. It's about leader credibility. Leaders need to meet and, hopefully, exceed expectations.

NBA basketball stars John Stockton, Shaquille O'Neal and Karl Malone have each created their own unique style of play. They respect superstar Michael Jordan but don't follow Jordan's style, focus or brand of basketball.

Because it requires an intense commitment to excellence, vision, innovation and a constant resolution to raise-the-bar productivity, leadership is often a lonely activity.

The more a person, company or product leader succeeds and soars, the more they are oftentimes resented by those around them for their success (subordinates, co-workers, competitors, etc.). Call it jealousy or envy, there is always animosity directed toward a leader. If only companies and individuals would take the vast amount of energy they waste on leader-directed negativism and channel it into positive growth-oriented action, they, one day, might enjoy greater success and perhaps grow into leadership themselves.

Again using an "MJ" (Michael Jordan) example, it all boils down to the marketing jingle once used by Gatorade to market their line of sports beverages: "I want to be like Mike!"

Don't you see? You can't be like Mike! You have to be like you!

———— ◇ ————

**Celebrate your uniqueness. Nurture your own
wonderful points of sustainable, discernible difference.**

———— ◇ ————

Everyone wants to be a leader, however, "wanting" is not enough. Dr. Price Pritchett wrote in his fabulous book, *You²*, "...wishing, longing, wanting, desiring...these are not the same as pursuing...they are essentially passive. Pursuit, on the other hand, is active." [11] Trusting in the power of pursuit is an important first step in rising to a position of leadership in a career or for a company or with a product.

Leadership *must* be pursued if it is to be achieved. It doesn't just happen, nor do positions of leadership simply fall into one's hands. Leading executives, companies and products all invariably entered into hot pursuit of specific objectives.

Learn from the leaders. Use them as models to help craft a unique career path and work style, a unique company positioning, posture and culture, or a unique line of meaningful products.

I once held the position of divisional president for a Chicago-based company called Rymer Foods. When initially interviewing for the position, I spent time with the company's chairman, Barry Rymer. Employed at the time of the interview by a division of Sara Lee, I was conditioned to expect certain things from companies. Why? Simply put, Sara Lee was a leader and I expected every viable company to do the kinds of things leaders do.

I was puzzled by the fact that Rymer Foods, at the time grossing about $300 million a year in sales and listed on the New York Stock Exchange, had no corporate brochure, no marketing materials, no catalogue and no product fact sheets. After all, each division of my then-current employer, Sara Lee, had piles and piles of high-gloss marketing materials to help support sales. I figured that if a leader like Sara Lee invested in all that paper, shouldn't everyone? Shouldn't Rymer?

I asked Barry, "How is it possible that your company does more than $300 million dollars in sales, yet you have absolutely no printed materials?"

His response was short, sweet, a bit sarcastic, to the point and characteristic of every entrepreneur who ever created his own business dynasty by not "following the leader" and traditional methodology: "Hey, what can I tell you? I was just too damn busy growing my business into a profitable $300 million company to spend any time developing pretty little printed brochures."

LEARN FROM LEADERS BUT DO IT YOUR OWN WAY

What's truly important is the learning, not necessarily the following. If an enterprise mirrors its activities after common leadership traits, one day that enterprise may have a chance at leading.

Why reinvent the wheel? Leadership has patterns.

For instance, leaders ignore criticism and attacks. Leaders look upon anything but constructive, helpful criticism as jealous negative reinforcement. Einstein wouldn't tolerate negativism. In fact, he once said, "Great spirits have always encountered violent opposition from mediocre minds."

Leaders very well may have to ignore criticism and lots of negative noise. Celebrated actor Danny Thomas ("Make Room For Daddy," etc.), once told me, "If you want to be leader of the orchestra, then you'll have to turn your back on the crowd."

——— ◇ ———

Leaders are also willing to accept failure, but more importantly, they learn from failure. After all, when you're through learning…you're through!

——— ◇ ———

When selecting key leaders for their "Most Admired Corporations" listing, *Fortune* Magazine[12] defined their selection criteria as:

- Quality of Management
- Use of Corporate Assets
- Talent and Motivation
- Innovation and Vision
- Quality of Products and Services
- Financial Soundness
- Innovativeness
- Value As A Long-Term Investment
- Community and Environmental Responsibility

In 1996 and 1997, companies that measured up to this criteria included Coca-Cola, Procter & Gamble, Mirage Resorts, Rubbermaid, Merck, UPS, Microsoft, Intel, Johnson & Johnson, Pfizer, Berkshire Hathaway, Hewlett-Packard and Motorola.

Study them. Learn from them.

——— ◇ ———

Leaders don't focus on effort. They obsess with results. Leadership, therefore, is not about position or positioning; it's about performance.

——— ◇ ———

Leaders are also ferociously bold competitive animals. Ray Kroc, the founder of McDonald's, once said, "It is ridiculous to call this an industry. This is dog eat dog. Rat eat rat. I've got to kill them before they kill me. You're talking about the American way...survival of the fittest."

Leaders represent a "mixed bag" of traits and core competencies all blended together to form a dynamo who accepts nothing less than success.

- Leaders put forth extra effort.
- Leaders try to be flexible.
- Leaders know when to take risks.
- Leaders have vision.
- Leaders believe in constantly learning.
- Leaders are both resourceful and creative.
- Leaders know when to be serious and when to have a sense of humor.
- Leaders try hard to maintain a positive attitude.
- Leaders know "how" and "when" to delegate.
- Leaders constantly work on improving their communication skills.
- Leaders are teachers, trainers, mentors and motivators.
- Leaders are both dreamers and realists wrapped up in one person.
- Leaders are relatively well-organized and generally decisive.
- Leaders readily encourage, extend praise and share success.
- Leaders are not afraid to fail.

So, should you follow a specific leader? No! Nonsense! Should you learn from specific leaders? Yes. Good sense!

If you truly study leaders and learn from leadership examples, you'll find many similar patterns to emulate. For example, leaders (companies, people) understand the incredible magic of morale and the power of positivism. "Passion" is also a very common trait in leading companies and people. Leaders are passionate about their vision, mission, industry, products, services, unique approaches to business, positioning, team (personnel) and even customers.

Leaders also regularly demonstrate "an attitude of gratitude" and appropriately acknowledge (and reward) achievement, contribution and team effort.

They have a keen understanding about the likely and logical changes on their business horizon and manage change well.

Leaders, whether they're people, companies or products, make a difference—period! They follow roads "less traveled on" often.

———— ◇ ————

There is also an inherent understanding that leadership *requires* a constant raise-the-bar attitude. History becomes unimportant.

———— ◇ ————

When I was an incoming freshman at the University of Maryland, I received a note from my soon-to-be Lacrosse coach, John "Hezzie" Howard, requesting each player to attend a "get-acquainted" meeting. The coach asked that each of us bring photocopies to the meeting of the very best newspaper articles and clippings from our high school Lacrosse careers.

We were under the impression that Coach Howard was going to pass along the articles to the University Sports Information Office so that they could craft press releases and articles on our incoming Class of '69. You see, our coach was confident that our team would ultimately be a national contender (we were Co-National Champs in 1967), and he wanted these articles to be used to promote the excellent crop of athletes who selected Maryland as their school. This, ultimately, could be an asset to help attract new players and bolster future recruiting efforts.

I'll never forget that first team meeting. After collecting our article copies, one of the coaches smiled at us, shoved the clippings into a trash can, lit a match and burned the articles. He then turned toward the players and screamed at us—a scream and words I'll never forget. "Nice articles, guys. However, here...your history means nothing!"

Decades later, I learned, first hand, that it's not just "here" that your history means nothing. It's everywhere!

Leaders understand that they've got to succeed every new day, in fact, every week, month, quarter and year.

Sure, feel great about your history. "High-five" past victories and accomplishments but never forget that leaders, though proud of their past achievements and heritage, obsess with "doing it again," perhaps even doing it better than in previous efforts.

I have had the benefit of a friendship with Mike Ilitch, an incredible business leader, who is the founder and chairman of Little Caesar Pizza, the owner of the NHL Detroit Red Wings and also owner of major league baseball's Detroit Tigers.

Both of my sons, Eric and Jeffrey, experienced "throwing out the first pitch" in different Tigers baseball games. What a thrill it was for both the boys and me. In fact, I'll never forget leaving what turned out to be a funny, yet "Freudian slip" voice message to my wife, Kim, on our answering machine after Eric threw out the ceremonial first pitch before that Tigers versus Brewers game in 1995: "Honey, this was the greatest experience...the greatest thrill ever in the life of a nine-year-old and his son!"

"A nine-year-old and his son?" Talk about an excited Dad...

The following year, in 1996, younger son Jeffrey threw out the pre-game pitch before a Tigers versus Baltimore Orioles contest. Prior to the game, we had the opportunity to spend some time on the field meeting a number of the players, as well as legendary manager Sparky Anderson.

The highlight of the activity for us, however, was our observation of Oriole infielder Cal Ripkin, Jr. who, before the game, hit about 150 balls off a rubber baseball tee into a net. Swat after swat, hit after hit, he practiced long and hard, batting each ball soundly off the tee into a restraining net.

It was interesting to watch the focus and intensity of this record-breaking, perennial All-Star leader. We found it even more interesting (and enlightening) to learn that Ripkin hit anywhere from 150-200 baseballs off a batting tee before every major league baseball game he had ever played for nearly seventeen years in the big leagues.

The question, "Why?" is easily answered.

Cal Ripkin, Jr., a player destined for the Hall of Fame, understood that leaders must constantly work on their game (or businesses or products or skills, etc.). Leaders work diligently on constantly improving and raising the bar on their performances. After all, one is only as good as his next hit!

Leaders also understand the power of people. Leader after successful leader, in all walks of life and in all kinds of businesses, demonstrates vital core competencies such as delegation skills, keen aptitudes for human resources, strong abilities to communicate and great insight in identifying qualified, proficient team members.

Identifying, qualifying and ultimately hiring solid team members for the "cause" is incredibly important. In fact, finding other superstar producers and thoroughbreds is also a skill many leaders master. A quote attributed to University of Oregon track coaching legend, Bill Bowerman, sums it up nicely, "If you want a track team to win the high jump, you find one person who can jump seven feet...not seven people who can jump one foot."

Some people (companies, products) make the cut...others fall by the wayside. Although there are common characteristics and traits of leaders, there's no magical formula.

Even leaders themselves find it difficult to convey what they did (and didn't do) to grab their respective pots of gold. J. Paul Getty sent the following response to a magazine reporter who requested that Getty explain his multibillion-dollar success in the petroleum business: "It's simple. Some people find oil. Others don't."

Learn from leaders. Live the pattern of leadership. Commit your career, business and products to becoming a leader, nothing less. Make the act and activity of leading a habit.

Rose Fitzgerald Kennedy wrote, "Superior achievement, or making the most of one's capabilities, is to a very considerable degree a matter of habit. This was the reason why Joe (husband Joseph Kennedy) used to say to the children, 'We don't want any losers around here. In this family, we want winners.' They were always encouraged to be winners, leaders and victors in whatever they set their hand to...and to develop the habit." (the children were Joe, Jr. a World War II decorated hero; John F. Kennedy, President of the United States; Robert Kennedy, U.S. Secretary of State; Edward (Ted) Kennedy, a State Senator; Eunice Kennedy Shriver, the founder and Chairperson of the Special Olympics and co-founder of the Peace Corps),

If you follow and imitate a specific leader and try to act exactly like that leader (be it a person, company or product offering), you'll likely not succeed. Instead, use leadership learning, mold the clay and craft your own sculpture—your very own brand of "leader."

———— ◇ ————

If everyone thinks alike, somebody isn't thinking.

———— ◇ ————

Don't "follow the leader." Learn from leaders, develop the habit of leadership and chart your own wonderful, unique course.

Lead on!

Challenge the Myths of Your Own Conventional Wisdom...

CHAPTER HIGHLIGHTS

- Most great works of art, industry and science came about because someone looked at the world differently.

- When it comes to leaders, there will never be "another," however, there can always be an "other."

- "Following the leader" is a great kids' game, but in business it is a myth that will likely get a company (and a career) into trouble.

- Celebrate your uniqueness. Nurture your own wonderful points of sustainable, discernible difference.

- Leadership *must* be pursued if it is to be achieved. It doesn't just happen nor do positions of leadership simply fall into one's hands.

- *Fortune* Magazine's "Most Admired Corporations" list defines their selection criteria as:
  - ◇ Quality of Management
  - ◇ Use of Corporate Assets
  - ◇ Talent and Motivation
  - ◇ Innovation and Vision
  - ◇ Quality of Products and Services
  - ◇ Financial Soundness
  - ◇ Innovativeness
  - ◇ Value as a Long-Term Investment
  - ◇ Community and Environmental Responsibility

- Leaders don't focus on effort. They are obsessed with results. Leadership, therefore, is not about position or positioning; it's about performance.
- Passion is also a common trait in outstanding companies and people. Leaders are passionate about their vision, mission, industry, products, services, unique approaches to business positioning, team (personnel) and even customers.
- There is also an inherent understanding that leadership *requires* a constant raise-the-bar attitude. History becomes unimportant.
- Make the act and activity of leading a habit.
- If everyone thinks alike, somebody isn't thinking.

◇

BIGGER IS BETTER!

I've heard people say, "BIG is beautiful!" Still, beautiful doesn't mean better. I also find it ironic that although BIGGER isn't necessarily BETTER, oftentimes BETTER will become BIGGER.

WE'RE IN DOWNSIZED, PERSONAL-SIZED, MINIATURIZED TIMES

Perhaps taking the lead from comedian Steve Martin's phrase, "Let's get small!" businesses all over the world are targeting a tighter, more cost-effective positioning. They have many names for the activity: "miniaturization," "right-sizing," "downsizing," "back-to-basics," "streamlining," "compression," "amalgamation," "restructuring," "consolidation" and more. To me, it's simply "cutting back."

That's not to say that "cutting back" or any of the other business terms used for it are bad. It's a reality of our business life. Do more with less.

Technology has given us computers that are smaller than a dime, telephones that fit in our pocket, color televisions that sit nicely in the palm of our hand and an entire encyclopedia on a microchip tinier than a Tic-Tac mint.

We understand the power of "micro"....in technology.

We understand just how mighty "small" can be....in equipment.

Many business people, however, still are obsessed with "BIG" when it comes to company size, myopically believing that BIG eventually wins.

Our world is filled with BIG companies, such as Con Agra, Kodak, General Motors, IBM, General Electric, Microsoft and others. Many of these mega-companies are so overbearing, so incredibly BIG that they dominate categories, even entire industries.

Yet, size alone doesn't necessarily lead to victory.

Big Xerox was riding high in 1972 as one of the twenty largest companies worldwide in terms of stock market valuation. Five years later, they fell off the list and have not regained that status since. Xerox's stock market value dropped from $11.8 billion in 1972 to less than $8.0 billion in 1993. They were losing share to smaller companies, including foreign competitors, plus their products were viewed as being of poor quality.

When taking over Xerox leadership in the mid-1980s, CEO David Kearns openly voiced his concern that big, powerful, once-undisputed leader Xerox was in danger of going out of business. Kearns has said, "We were becoming a dinosaur that couldn't get out of its own way."

The good news, however, is that under Kearns' leadership, and with a massive repositioning program (i.e., new focus on quality, new energy geared toward copy machine market leadership, new programs, etc.), big Xerox is back on the "better" side of the ledger sheet and thriving. This is yet another example that indicates how big companies can falter if they lose focus and start believing their own press clippings.

Oh, by the way, big—very big—General Motors recorded the single largest loss ever to hit a Fortune 500 Company when, in 1992, the mammoth automotive manufacturer posted a loss in excess of $23.5 billion. Obviously, bigger doesn't necessarily mean more profitable, either.

Imagine for a moment the surprise and shock that Procter & Gamble, Kraft General Foods and Nestle must have experienced in the sleepy grocery shelf category called "coffee" when Starbucks slam-dunked (no coffee pun intended) its young, upstart brand into the position of category dominance.

P&G is a BIG, multibillion dollar company. Kraft General Foods is a BIG, multibillion dollar company. Nestle is real BIG. In fact, in

1996, they were the largest food company in the world, earning in excess of $62.0 billion.

Call them Goliaths. Call them giants. Call them BIG! Call them asleep at the wheel, perhaps.

Starbucks *was* a little coffee roasting company based in Seattle, Washington. They marketed fresh ground roasted coffee as *real* coffee to the dismay of P&G (Taster's Choice), Kraft (International Coffees) and Nestle (Nescafe, Chase & Sanborn)—all mega-marketers of soluble coffee (better known as "instant").

Starbucks bundled retail theater, aroma, great graphics, pretty trade dress—and they also targeted high-traffic locations (airports, arenas, bus terminals, college campuses, malls, in-flight food services, etc.) as opposed to the highly competitive, "me, too" grocery shelf distribution channel.

They also have aggressively extended their brand reach and presence through a dynamic ubiquity strategy.

It's difficult to find BIGGER food companies than P&G, KGF and Nestle.

Still, little Starbucks (relatively speaking) reinvented coffee marketing and, in the eyes of the consumer, Starbucks has become the definition of coffee.

Hence, they were BETTER in their business-building than their BIGGER old line competitors.

Interestingly enough, Starbucks also focused on a different type of "BIG" positioning. Their version of "big," however, didn't relate to size. It related to ideas. Their broad-based business development approach was a "big idea." Their targeted points of distribution strategy (a ubiquity strategy similar to Coca-Cola's) was obviously another "big idea."

Whether a company is BIG or small, there always will be a need for BIG business-building approaches, but that doesn't mean programs have to come in BIG packages.

After all, the only size that matters is the size of customer satisfaction achieved. To reiterate, the *only* size that matters is the size of customer satisfaction achieved.

Quality output is more important than big output and production. Ralph Waldo Emerson wrote, "The true test of a civilization is not the census nor the size of the cities nor the size of the crop production...but the kind of man that the country turns out."

This speaks to quality. Regardless of size, quality ultimately wins. Big or small, it is the quality mindset, whether in operations, products, programs, people, communication, innovation, execution and in attention to detail (big and small) that takes enterprises to the top.

———◇———

**Big companies that stay on top, ironically enough,
have to constantly focus on the smallest detail.
It's an interesting blend of "big" and "small."**

———◇———

Wal-Mart is a prime example. As "big" as Wal-Mart has become, they still aggressively direct management efforts at the smallest detail, component and lowest common denominator. David Glass, Wal-Mart's Chief Executive Officer, said, "If someone asks me how we manage a $100 billion company, I tell them a store at a time, and we constantly challenge that unit to make it the best."

Challenging each small component and element that makes up the big enterprise is one reason why giant Wal-Mart stays on top of both its industry and its game. Its "big" corporate headquarters, in Bentonville, Arkansas, actually listens to its "small" units. When a specific store uncovers a new way to market or sell a category, program or product, there are communication vehicles designed to share that idea with both the system and the corporate headquarters. This culture of constant sharing keeps good ideas flowing, communication fluid and everyone energized, bottom to top, and vice versa. Over the years, many important Wal-Mart ideas came from the field.

In 1993, I had the opportunity to attend one of Wal-Mart's famous Saturday morning pep rallies at corporate headquarters. The pep rallies are weekly team meetings held both at corporate headquarters and in each individual store. They are designed for communication. Ideas, information, successes, failures, updates, "high-five" celebrations and more take place at these free-wheeling, highly spirited meetings, which convey a near cult-like fervor.

The key to the pep rally system is its incredibly high level of communication. That's one way "big" Wal-Mart remains "better."

It's unusual for an "outsider" to attend a Wal-Mart pep rally at their corporate offices, however, my associates from Coca-Cola Fountain and I were being honored by Wal-Mart and were invited by Tom Coughlin, then a Wal-Mart Senior Vice-President, for a food court program we developed for ten Wal-Mart stores (called "Home Town Favorites"). I thought we were there to be observers, not participants. I expected Tom to acknowledge our presence and then move on to other business.

I was wrong.

Wal-Mart's culture simply doesn't tolerate "observers" at its meetings. If you attend, you participate.

In the true Wal-Mart spirit of sharing, Tom turned to Dick Flaig, Coca-Cola Fountain's Vice-President of National Accounts, and to me and asked each of us to "share" with the 500 headquarters' employees in attendance the key "learnings" from the food court initiative.

After addressing the group, we received questions from the floor and our remarks were ultimately printed in a communiqué that was sent to everyone in the entire Wal-Mart system. In my estimation, "big," better Wal-Mart, being obsessed with learning, sharing and communicating, will continue to grow and prosper.

Wal-Mart is obviously a "big" exception to "big" company patterns. Typically, large companies ignore the small details and ultimately flounder as a result of it.

Big mistake!

Big or small, companies must address details and be aggressive in their communication. This is obviously easier for a small- to mid-size company than for a giant.

Through it all, "big" is envied. Big is the ideal and the goal of so many business people.

The irony is that we are in a world that talks a lot about "miniaturizing," "downsizing," "right-sizing," and readily uses words like "micro," "byte," "bit," etc. It would seem that "big" would be an unpopular concept. Still, so many companies focus their efforts and direct their dreams at being "big."

We seem confused. Pocket calculators, personal-sized computers and compact cars are just three examples of how we embrace smaller, more efficient products.

Yet, we're still enamored by "big." Soft drinks are rarely marketed anymore as "Small," "Medium" and "Large." Instead, they're labeled "Large," "Giant" and "Super-Size." Bulk packaging is an important retail strategy. Club stores sell items by the pallet as opposed to the piece. We're infatuated with big screen TVs, stretch limousines and jumbo jets. Big, big and bigger—we're living on a want-it-all-in-big-chunks planet.

Look up and down the streets of your town.

Butcher shops, bakeries, corner candy stores, floral shops, local pharmacies, liquor stores and banks—all once part of the fabric of America's small business landscape—have slowly but surely moved from their small freestanding locations into one-stop-shop big supermarkets. Now part of a bigger retailing environment, the assumption is that they're better.

Not necessarily.

Rolls Royce isn't the biggest car manufacturer in the world, however, they're considered one of the best. Year after year, their profits soar. Rolls Royce has become synonymous with quality, prestige and "better." Houston's Restaurants, a chain of fifty-plus casual dinner houses, is a much smaller chain than its competitors Applebee's, Bennigan's, Chili's and TGI Friday's, however, they annually receive better "grades" from consumers and percentage-wise, are more profitable than their competitors. When it comes to prepared foods, perishables and deli, Ukrop's Supermarkets, a "small" twenty-three unit operation in Richmond, Virginia, is considered both the most successful and the most innovative supermarket company in the U.S. Their competitors have hundreds, even thousands, of stores. Ukrop's surely isn't bigger. They're better!

In the words of Supreme Court Justice William O. Douglas, "The growth of bigness has resulted in ruthless sacrifices of human values. The disappearance of free enterprise has submerged the individual in the impersonal corporation. When a nation of shopkeepers is transformed into a nation of big store clerks, enormous spiritual sacrifices are made."

This leads to my conclusion that unless bigness is managed, monitored and quality-controlled (like Wal-Mart), businesses obsessed with bigness will be in *big* trouble!

Look, anything to excess is bad. Uncontrolled bigness can result in a company that is impersonal, cold, detached, remote, indifferent, disinterested and downright stifling. The key is to control the growth and, simultaneously with the growth, maintain core competencies and discernible points of unique difference in order to constantly provide an incredibly high level of customer satisfaction. Controlled bigness is good.

Through it all, it can be fatal to ignore the power of small, tight, efficient companies. C. Jackson Grayson and Carla O'Dell in their book, *American Business: A Two-Minute Warning*,[13] ranked the No. 3 reason "why leaders fail and challengers rise to take their place," as this:

"Size!"

Leaders underestimate competitive strengths of small companies. They're too tiny to be a threat, they say. I believe there is a place for "big." However, my viewpoint on "big" is not related to the size of an enterprise but the size of its efficiency, viability, execution, profitability, customer satisfaction and passion.

Believing we should all be "change catalysts," I am also convinced that change should be big and bold.

Big "anything" can be intimidating, scary, awesome, impressive and even breathtaking. Big is often powerful. Big has seemingly unlimited resources and big is "supposed" to crush little.

MYTH! MYTH!

Don't forget that big companies are often bureaucratic, inflexible, headstrong, obstinate, rigid, stubborn and clumsy.

Just as biblical history recounts the story of David conquering Goliath, business history books are filled with case studies of small companies that overturned and destroyed giant corporations.

Many of these once small companies grew to become big, powerful leaders, however, they protected their position of excellence by consistently practicing those activities that led them to growth. To paraphrase an old rural expression, they never forgot who or what brought them to the dance.

Ray Kroc's few hundred McDonald's restaurants challenged Howard Johnson's 1,000 units. The much smaller McDonald's organization ultimately won because they operated their restaurants better, managed their costs better, motivated their personnel better, marketed their menu better and communicated value to the consumer better. Ultimately, the Ho Jo giant toppled. In 1997,

Howard Johnson's operated a few hundred hotels and about fifty restaurants. McDonald's, on the other hand, operates 15,000 restaurants and has served "billions and billions" of hamburgers to its customers worldwide. "Big" companies that aren't "better" will ultimately crash and burn.

Green Bay, Wisconsin is a city whose population was approximately 158,000 in 1967. That very same year, New York had a population of approximately 11,500,000; Chicago had a population of about 7,000,000 and Los Angeles a population of approximately 5,200,000. While New York, Chicago and Los Angeles were BIG, powerful cities and considered superb media markets and terrific pro sports towns, Green Bay was a small, poor media market and by all rights, shouldn't even have had an NFL team.

Both Green Bay's franchise size and its relatively small-city pro sports income made it very difficult for the Packers to afford anything but a modest player-personnel budget. Nonetheless, through positioning, franchise management, unique civic ownership of the club, team leadership and on-the-field execution, the Packers won both their NFL division championship and Super Bowl I in 1967. For years to follow, Green Bay remained a pro football powerhouse with a proud "winning" tradition (in the box office, on the field and throughout its ledger pages). Their business acumen and quality product helped this David topple big city Goliaths.

Big companies are usually strapped with heavy, oftentimes burdensome baggage.

This "baggage" (represented by size) affects communication, reaction time and a consistent vision throughout its system.

The larger an organization, the more apt they are to become and to operate as a bureaucracy. Needless to say, without proper controls, leadership and an "*intre*preneurial" spirit, bureaucracies are prone to rigidity, inflexibility, apathy, departmental protectionism, silos, fiefdoms and a lack of innovation.

It is precisely because of these bureaucratic gaps that smaller, more agile companies can react, act and capitalize on quick-to-close windows of opportunity better than the big guys. After all, big companies are typically focused on systems, rules, regulations, procedures and policies—and they seem to put all process-related items before action. Stockpiling bulletins, rule books, directives, memos and manuals seems to take precedence over stockpiling an arsenal filled with weapons of business war. Also, policymakers seem to be more important than business development foot soldiers.

There's also a coldness about big business. People are reduced to being referred to as "desks" and the very same human spirit, energy and passion that contributed to a company's growth is quickly forgotten and often suppressed when a company gets to be big.

Big companies need spirit, individualism and creativity, too. These vital activities shouldn't stop once a company becomes large. To stay on top, there's a need to be more energetic than ever before. Arriving at the top of the hill doesn't ensure permanent tenancy of either the property or the position. After all, if you become static, as opposed to dynamic, there's only one place to go when you're big and on top of the world. And that one place is surely not a preferred destination.

Just as little Starbucks made a successful run for coffee market share leadership once held by giants Kraft, Nestle and P&G, little Southwest Airlines wrestled large chunks of air travel dollars away from multibillion dollar carriers like American, Delta and United. How? Southwest performed better. They didn't focus on the size of their airline. Their singular focus was on the size of passenger satisfaction.

Once upon a time, Nike was little. Its competitors, Converse, Keds and PF Flyers were huge marketing machines, but Nike marketed, merchandised, positioned, promoted and sold their wares better, ultimately becoming bigger. Swoosh!

General Motors' Saturn model was a little automobile brand competing in an industry filled with old line, *big* power brands. Providing better value, better engine efficiency, better design and better ideas for consumers, Saturn grew to the position of market dominance.

Waging war against the big, powerful Japanese small car manufacturers that owned commanding market leadership in the U.S., Saturn didn't just come up with a better car. Instead, the Saturn Company created a new car manufacturing structure. Operating as an autonomous company separate from parent General Motors, it aggressively focused resources on new-wave robotics and technology. It obsessively nurtured active employee involvement through empowerment. It invested heavily in each community it operated in. It developed a unique marketing program that offered "individualized attention" through customer service consultants.

Saturn redesigned the typical organization chart to make it more employee- and team-directed than is the more traditional top-down structure.

I cringe when I hear marketing people talk about "bigger ideas." I get excited when I hear someone talk about "better ideas." Before even thinking about getting any bigger, companies need to spend time (and resources) on how they can become (and stay) better.

"Better" is the key word here.

"Bigger" is fine, but only if a company is also "better."

Challenge the Myths of Your Own Conventional Wisdom...

CHAPTER HIGHLIGHTS

- We're in downsized, personal-sized, miniaturized times.
- It's a reality of our business life. Do more with less.
- Size alone doesn't necessarily lead to victory.
- Big companies that stay on top, ironically enough, have to constantly focus on the smallest detail. It's an interesting blend of "big" and "small."
- Anything to excess is bad.
- Bigger isn't necessarily better, yet "better" becomes bigger.
- I cringe when I hear marketing people talk about "bigger ideas." I get excited when I hear discussion of "better ideas."
- Before even thinking about getting any bigger, companies need to spend time (and resources) on how they can become (and stay) better.
- Better is the key word here. Bigger is fine, but only if a company also is "better."

◇

MYTH FIVE

GOOD FENCES MAKE GOOD NEIGHBORS

After studying many of the enterprises featured in *Fortune* Magazine's "America's Most Admired Companies"[14] issues, over the years, I started to notice an intriguing pattern: Each and every CEO and chairperson of these "most admired" organizations energetically maintained the belief that an important key to business development was engagement in strategic alliances.

Sure, some executives called the strategy "searching for business building synergies," others called it "seeking symbiotic relationships," still others referred to it as "partnering." Nonetheless, they were all saying the same thing. There is clearly strength in numbers!

Could Merck, UPS, Intel, Hewlett-Packard, Pfizer, Mirage Resorts, Johnson & Johnson, Rubbermaid and Home Depot be wrong? Were their key executives so focused on courses in business, finance, technology and economics in their younger days that they never took an American literature class in college and read Robert Frost's wonderful poem, "Mending Wall"?[15] If they had, they might have been convinced that "good fences make good neighbours" and might have avoided anything that even closely resembled cooperating with other companies.

Obviously, Coca-Cola's alliance with McDonald's; Motorola's alliance with Toshiba; Microsoft's alliance with Apple computers and other examples fly directly in the face of Frost's neighbor who, in the poem, was obviously a proponent of separatism.

Assuming the viewpoint of the verse, that good fences, in actuality, do not make good neighbors, Frost wrote, "Something there is that doesn't love a wall, that wants it down..."

Anyone conducting business in a time of stress, turmoil, complexity and high-velocity change should understand the need for allies and the importance of collaboration. After all, fences separate neighbors, companies and careers—and serve as barriers to growth.

The key to business development, especially in a complex, highly competitive time, is *not* separatism. Instead, it is collaboration, open communication, affiliation, association, partnering and strategic alliances. Good fences block out neighbors who otherwise might become important allies and associates. Good fences block out the light. And just as light is the scientific key to natural growth, it is also a key to career, business and product growth and prosperity.

"Something there is that doesn't love a wall..."

Business is much too dizzy, busy and complicated for any one company (or employee) to be "all things to all people." It is illogical for any one enterprise to claim expertise and competency, for instance, in Finance, Management, Marketing, Merchandising, Sales, Promotion, Public Relations, Management Information Systems, Human Resources, Fully-Integrated Production, Distribution, Logistics, Packaging, Consumer Trends, International Marketing, etc. Yet, successful business ventures (or adventures, as I frequently call them) require expertise in all of the above—and in every functional area.

Businesses cannot afford *not* to be versatile and competent in lots of areas. Realistically, most businesses have gaps and surely could benefit from added expertise and assistance in a number of development and functional areas. Breaking down the fences and putting in some free-swinging doors (or windows of opportunity) by building alliances with companies that are compatible can only lead to developmental success.

After all, the major benefits derived from strategic alliances are powerful. They are:

1. Value

2. Efficiency

3. Information

4. Education

5. Risk Reduction

6. Expert Input

7. Association

8. Growth

Who could argue the importance of that list? Sure seems to me that each of the aforementioned benefits offer willing partners ways to enhance each of their operations, improve productivity, extend brand reach, leverage new opportunities through powerful associations, build business and achieve new competitive advantages.

So, what is a "strategic alliance?"

A strategic alliance is a multifaceted business association between two or more successful, solvent and compatible enterprises that requires each to possess:

- an inclination toward sharing,
- a predisposition toward honest communication,
- a proclivity for receiving objective assistance,
- a willingness to allocate resources toward a common goal,
- a penchant for participation and association,
- an enthusiasm for the mutual transfer of knowledge,
- a propensity for open cooperation and collaboration, and
- once again, an inclination toward sharing (which is worthy of repeating).

Each company in an alliance must make ongoing and equal contributions to the alliance; each must bring to the alliance special skills, assets, contacts, technology, access, information, expertise and core competencies. And each company in an alliance must be a capable catalyst to create new value for all parties involved.

———◇———

No alliance member can be dominant.
All parties must be strong, solvent and successful.

———◇———

Each partner's individual pattern and history of success is important. Successful alliances are not alliances between weak companies and strong companies. They are alliances between the strong and the strong. Being cooperative is simply not enough. When a strong company aligns itself with a weak company, the imbalance brings a great deal of anxiety and stress to the association.

Considering this, I'm reminded of a line of philosophy from that great 20th century philosopher, Woody Allen, in his hit movie "Annie Hall."[16] Allen, discussing relationships, alluded to the fact that although a lion can lie down with a lamb, the lamb likely will not get much sleep.

The same holds true for prospective alliance partners. The reality is that lions and lambs cannot coexist. Alliances between strong and weak parties simply do not work. Consider alliances as more than business "deals," more than just "transactions." Their essence consists of more than just sharing tidbits of intellectual property.

Strategic alliances also are more than sophisticated. Outsourcing, after all, is transferring internal activities to an external supplier. It's letting "the other guy" handle their specialty area while you focus on your own core competencies.

Strategic partnerships are more than that.

A strategic alliance must absolutely fit the vision, mission and guiding principles of each alliance member.

In order for an alliance to succeed, each company must have similar corporate cultures, similar viewpoints on corporate ethics, similar operating styles, individual objectives that are similar and in sync, comparable types of management, similar definitions of success and, as previously noted, an individual pattern and history of success.

There must be interdependence. Mutual need creates a viable alliance. Each company, though interdependent in each specific strategic alliance, must be independently successful and solid.

Obviously, each company in an alliance must trust its partner(s).

No trust? No teamwork!

All parties in an alliance must view the alliance as important. In fact, if the top executives in a company either are not actively involved in the alliance or are not totally supportive of the alliance, it will fail.

A regularly updated scorecard is paramount to an alliance's success. There need to be "performance requirements" in any strategic alliance. Tracking, measuring, analyzing and monitoring activities, efforts, initiatives, results and resource allocation are all vital. If the performance standards and objectives are not being realized, the transfer of knowledge, technology, contacts and expertise must be adjusted accordingly.

Alliances are not meant to be "good tries." Increased sharing among partners should be the outcome of the initiative. Success should be defined by results, not "just" strong efforts.

From utilizing a shared one-stop-shop approach to supply and service; to dramatically cutting learning curves on new technology; from adapting to new market conditions and changes faster; to borrowing another's expertise and intellectual property; from adding complementary capacity to building operational synergies...and on and on and on...strategic alliances offer all kinds of business-building benefits.

Whether it be collaborative selling, co-distribution, design coordination, cooperative advertising, licensed technology, subcontracted research or another strategy, there is truly strength in numbers.

Interestingly, accounting and consulting giant Coopers & Lybrand conducted a survey in late 1997, which concluded that of the nearly 500 small- and mid-size businesses interviewed, nearly half planned to engage in some sort of strategic partnership, alliance or joint venture in 1998. This figure was dramatically higher than survey results in each year since 1993, when Coopers & Lybrand began conducting the research.

Examples of such alliances include:

Netscape and Microsoft developing a framework for built-in privacy safeguards for the Internet.

The IBM and Federal Express alliance developed for service efficiency. IBM stocks important parts and components in Federal Express warehouses for faster than "just in time" fulfillment, service and supply. Federal Express, in turn, uses the IBM Consulting Group (ICG) to assist them in building more sophisticated systems.

It's the transportation alliance forged between the J.B. Hunt Company and the Santa Fe Railroad, two highly hostile competitors, which combined to form a delivered-to-your-door trucking service (Hunt) and the cost-efficiencies associated with long-distance over-the-rail transporting (Santa Fe). Hunt trucks were loaded on Santa Fe flatbed train cars for a shared opportunity.

An interesting and innovative approach to utilizing a "strength in numbers" process for business development is the system devised by the Food Marketing Institute (FMI),[17] the grocery industry's key association. Realizing that many of their chain supermarket members across the United States had similar problems and were each addressing these problems differently, the FMI established a "share group" program. In short, the trade association matches and bundles four or five noncompetitive retailers from different parts of the United States and facilitates a share group quarterly meeting at a different group member's location to address common opportunities, threats, trends, etc. One calendar quarter the group might meet on a marketing-related issue....another quarter a distribution-related issue....still another quarter a session devoted to a range of pertinent subjects.

With the intent that each member openly and honestly "share" their viewpoints, solutions and action plans relating to each issue, these share groups have become enormously successful. In 1997 it was estimated that the FMI had assisted in the creation of nearly 100 operating groups. The FMI's "share group" system is proving to be an excellent business-building vehicle.

The example list goes on and on....

———◇———

If it can be conceived, it can be created!

—Albert Einstein

———◇———

Typically, alliances based on technology transfer and subject matter expertise (competence) are usually the most successful. However, providing partners and customers a wide variety of ideas and information, properly managed, can also prove very beneficial.

An alliance need not just be forged by two or more supply companies. A supplier can also benefit greatly by developing a business-development alliance with its customers. Call it offering "value-add," or call it a supplier-buyer strategic alliance, providing "and more," learning from each side of the supply chain can be invaluable for gaining growth ideas, information and actionable data, as well as helping suppliers and buyers build stronger bonds and an improved working relationship.

One of the Coca-Cola guiding principles I most admire is their so-called A.S.K. program. A.S.K. is an acronym for "Always Share Knowledge." Coke believes that above and beyond providing its customers with good products at a competitive price, they must also work to develop alliances with customers by providing ongoing ideas, information, education and *always sharing knowledge*!

In every strategic partnership, ends must justify means. Each partner must work diligently to manage the relationship, not just the agreement. Each partner also must understand that strategic alliances tend to be living, ever-changing, ever-evolving business systems. New ways to work together offer endless possibilities.

What are the pitfalls? Why do some of these associations fail?

A company's fame, fortune and history, often coupled with pride and ego, can be a stumbling block to alliance success. I find it ironic that the same steppingstone we might use to walk a path can also be a stumbling block if we're not careful how we walk.

On the other hand, a company's fame, fortune and history can also be an enormous asset to an alliance's credibility and growth, provided associational business-building efforts are extended.

Obviously, there need to be wide open communication channels, regularly scheduled business reviews and empowered employees dedicated to managing the alliance if it's going to work.

Some alliances fail because one of the partners becomes reluctant to continue taking and using another partner's expertise. There should be no feeling of guilt about the transfer process. Exchanging ideas, resources, intelligence, education, actionable data and valuable contacts represents the foundation of an alliance's value. Exchange is the whole point of a strategic alliance. Eventually, each alliance member will have its chance to reciprocate and be on the giving end of the continuum. Alliances are based on give and take. The alliance will be ineffectual if one partner is shy about taking or hesitant about giving. There is no room for a competitive spirit among strategic partners. A spirit of sharing is vital.

Still, others fail because of unrealistic alliance objectives, uneven commitment and energy levels—and even cultural differences too wide to bridge. Managing trade-offs can be difficult, at best.

Based on caring, daring and openly sharing, strategic alliances offer openminded businesses a strength-in-numbers approach to business building.

———◇———

The bold endgame attitude an alliance should convey to the
world-at-large comes forth as both a challenge and question:
"How would *you* like to compete against *us*?"

———◇———

Whether you call this phenomenon an alliance, partnership, union, coalition, bloc, affiliation, ally, cohort, friendship, confederation, connection, association or gang, business building is based on many things, including the creation, focused development, nurturing and management of a well-defined network. Highly appropriate to our times, networking has become a crucial strategy in our modern, high-tech world.

Still, as much as alliances and business development oriented networks make sense, many executives are reluctant to enter into working agreements with other companies. It takes a very open mind to collaborate, share and embrace alliance-building. Don't forget about the parachute!

Businesses are too complicated *not* to consider developing strategic partnerships. This is not just about sharing technology or contacts. Consider this a way to amass brain power through a highly effective alliance decision-making process. Each member of the alliance brings its own ideas, information, education, experience, expertise, data, frame of reference and input. Each member also likely represents divergent thinking, which can lead to many additional viewpoints and alternatives. There's a kind of safety net derived from group decision-making (and action). It makes for a dynamic program based on both strength in numbers and safety in numbers.

Good fences do not, in fact, make good business neighbors.

Open up the gates of opportunity. Creatively use contacts. Network! Build all kinds of integrated alliances. I, for one, believe in all shapes and forms of alliances and ascribe to the networking philosophy that "...success is directly related to the size of your Rolodex," or more appropriately, the amount of entries in your Panasonic Business Card Scanner. Truly, there is "strength in numbers!"

Challenge the Myths of
Your Own Conventional Wisdom...

CHAPTER HIGHLIGHTS

- Clearly, there is strength in numbers.

- The key to business development, especially in a complex, highly competitive time, is *not* separatism. It is collaboration, open communication, affiliation, association, partnering and strategic alliances.

- Business is much too dizzy, busy and complicated for any one company (or employee) to be all things to all people.

- The major benefits derived from strategic alliances are powerful and include the following:
  - ◇ Value
  - ◇ Efficiency
  - ◇ Information
  - ◇ Education
  - ◇ Risk Reduction
  - ◇ Expert Input
  - ◇ Association
  - ◇ Growth

- A strategic alliance is a multifaceted business association between two or more successful, solvent and compatible enterprises that requires each member of the alliance to possess: an inclination toward sharing, a predisposition toward honest communication, a proclivity for receiving objective assistance, a willingness to allocate resources toward a common goal, a penchant for participation and association, an enthusiasm for the mutual transfer of knowledge, and a propensity for open cooperation and collaboration.

- No alliance member can be dominant. All parties must be strong, solvent and successful.

- Alliances are more than business "deals" and more than just "transactions."

- In order for an alliance among companies to succeed, the companies must have:
  - ◇ similar corporate cultures

- ◊ similar viewpoints on corporate ethics
- ◊ similar operating styles
- ◊ individual objectives that are similar and in sync
- ◊ comparable types of management;
- ◊ similar definition of success
- ◊ an individual pattern and history of success.
- No trust? No teamwork!
- There needs to be "performance requirements" in any strategic alliance.
- Success is directly correlative to the size of your Rolodex (or your Panasonic).

◊

THE FIRST ONE "IN" WINS

Being "first" can be a positive thing.

It feels "good" to be first and it certainly feels good to feel good.

However, being first may not necessarily be the best place to be with certain business-building initiatives and definitely does not ensure long-lasting success and a position of leadership.

Yes, history remembers "firsts" but is not often kind to those pioneers who went from first to worst. Over the long term, history happily remembers (and is kind to) refined, improved, successful business models, regardless of how early in the game they introduced their concept, company or product line.

BEING BEST IS BETTER THAN BEING FIRST

Orville and Wilbur Wright own a major piece of history for allegedly having been "first in flight" when their airplane lifted off at Kitty Hawk, North Carolina in 1903. Although we think of them as having been first, in reality, they were *not* the first to fly.

The list of inventors and adventurers who tried to soar with the eagles is long. In fact, there were many airplane experiments as far back as the early 1840s—the most notable being William Samuel Henson's and John Stringfellow's "flying machine" (named "The Aerial Steam Carriage" by the inventors). Then, in 1891, British-born Australian inventor, Lawrence Hargrave, flew his unmanned "flapping flyer" aircraft, whose wings "flapped like a bird," 312 feet.

Another American, astronomer Samuel Pierpont Langley, successfully launched his "Aerodome" craft in 1901—two years before the Wright Brothers made their memorable flight.

However, ask any twelve-year-old child to identify William Henson, John Stringfellow, Lawrence Hargrave or Samuel Langley and they'll draw a blank. Then ask the same child to identify the Wright Brothers and they'll quickly tell you all about Orville and Wilbur's history-making flight.

The Wright Brothers obviously won. They will forever be remembered as the leaders even though they were *not* the first ones "in" (or more appropriately, "up").

It was the distance flown, the time in flight and the capability of safely carrying a passenger that locked Orville and Wilbur into the history books, not the myth of first.

Why aren't we driving cars produced by Oliver Evans or Trevithick Motors on our highways and byways today instead of vehicles made by Ford? After all, American inventor Oliver Evans received his patent for a steam-propelled "auto" in 1789 and later produced the vehicle in 1803. By the same token, in 1801, scientist Richard Trevithick drove his engine-propelled carriage through the streets of London. Records talk of it being clumsy, smelly and noisy, yet it transported Trevithick and it *was* truly one of the first automobiles.

In 1885, German inventor Karl Benz developed a gasoline-powered vehicle. Later, in 1892, Charles Edgar Duryea and his brother Frank introduced their "horseless carriage," while German inventor Gottlieb Daimler's internal combustion carriage hit the streets of Munich in 1887.

The list of automobile pioneers is a virtual traffic jam backed up through the pages of history books.

Honk, honk! Into the passing lane motored Detroit's hero, Henry. In 1893, Henry Ford experimented with his "carriage" (abbreviated as "car") and called it the "Model T." Ford obviously wasn't first. Ford didn't care about being first. All he cared about was being best!

Precisely because his Model T was the best in a parking lot full of early autos, it is *best remembered* as the automotive leader and innovator. In addition, Ford's modernized manufacturing operation also represented an early (although not the first) example of automation and an assembly line approach to production. His cars were strong, reliable, efficient, attractive (by standards of the times), relatively easy to repair and, by 1908, his assembly line efficiency made cars inexpensive enough that ordinary people could afford to buy them.

Today, the global leader in film and photographic accessories is Eastman Kodak. Yet, Kodak was far from being the first one "in." One of the earliest-known examples of film production and usage for photography on record was in 1827 when French physicist Joseph Nicéphore Niépce presented his photographs (called "heliographs") to the French Academy of Science. He was followed by another Frenchman, Jacques Mande Daguerre, who in 1831 developed an entire photographic "process" of film development (referred to as "daguerrotype" images). Many others experimented and produced photographic products up until 1883, when George Eastman unveiled both his "box camera" and Kodak continuous strip film in a roll (with capacity for about 100 photos).

We know the rest of the story, of course. However, the key is that Kodak was better than its predecessors. Being "better" is better than being first. The list of "first one in" companies that suffered major misses is long.

Just as most people have forgotten that Univac was the first computer built (where are they now?), many of us forget that it was Xerox, not Apple, IBM or another high-tech company, that manufactured the very "first" personal computer. In fact, Xerox built this "first" PC nearly two years before any other company's model hit the streets.

Deciding that the computer business would be a nice "fit" to complement its copier business, Xerox established a Palo Alto Research Center (PARC), where it created the highly innovative "Alto," the Xerox brand name for its history-making PC (1975). Unfortunately, Xerox was bitten by the "first one in wins" myth, big time.

Everything went wrong!

For instance, the Xerox company assigned their copier sales personnel the responsibility of selling Alto. Having a history of difficulty selling any products other than copiers, the sales force failed miserably trying to launch Xerox personal computers. Secondly, the Xerox legal team strongly advised PARC scientists to fill out the necessary legal papers to safeguard Xerox's innovative PC technology, yet, somehow this was never done and no patents were prepared to protect the Alto process, system and hardware.

Needless to say, it became open season for all kinds of competitors to move in on the very vulnerable Xerox and legally imitate all aspects of its innovative new personal computer. In addition, many key Xerox executives didn't embrace the PC opportunity as important so they either held back financial support for PARC or allocated resources toward other ventures. Not surprisingly, Xerox's personal computer business evaporated.

Although Xerox is still credited with creating many of the most important breakthrough ideas that established a foundation for the personal computer industry, Xerox elected to limit its PC business to the production and supply of selected components, not personal computers.

Time for a drink? How 'bout something light and low cal?

The very first major diet soda on the market was Diet Rite Cola. It was first. It was also vile! Try to find it on your supermarket shelves today. It barely exists.

The global leader in diet colas today is clearly Diet Coke. By the way, Diet Coke was either the fifth or sixth national brand of low calorie colas to hit the marketplace. I'm sure you won't have any trouble finding this nearly ubiquitous product today. It's "everyanywhere"—but it wasn't first!

Avis was undaunted that rival Hertz was the "first one in" in the auto rental business. Obsessed with quality, consistency, value and service, Avis spent nearly twenty years advertising its direct marketing frontal attack against rival Hertz with a creative, "We're No. 2! We Try Harder!" campaign.

Car rental customers obviously liked the fact that Avis "tries harder." Voting with their dollars (more specifically "charge cards"), car rental customers embraced Avis' positioning and the company has been enjoying incredible success and growth. Why? Simply put, trying harder is a great quality. Trying harder is noble, good, solid, wholesome and viable.

———◇———

**And you don't have to be "first"
to try harder and be "best."**

———◇———

Football fans...the Cleveland Browns were an early entry into the NFL, certainly one of the "first" franchises to gain financial success while under their legendary leader, Paul Brown.

Today, in 1998, the City of Cleveland still stands. The Browns, unfortunately, do not. Back in 1995, the Browns closed their doors after a dismal decade of problems, including an inadequate stadium and the offer of a better deal to take up new residence in Baltimore (enter the Baltimore Ravens).

Yet, the Cleveland Browns had been one of football's premier NFL franchises. They're gone now. The good news for Cleveland is that there's a plan to revitalize the franchise and start over in 1999. Obviously, it's too late to be first anymore. Perhaps this time the Browns will work to be the best.

Once called "the five and dime," Woolworth was the very first major national discount department store chain in the U.S. Then came Sears, JCPenney, W.T. Grant, Ben Franklin Stores, Kmart, Wal-Mart, Target and others. Still, Woolworth was first, opening their doors in 1879. A place a shopper could get a shirt, a bottle of cough medicine, toys, food, even a goldfish, they were an expanded "general store"...a variety store and mass merchandiser like no other.

Years passed and market share dwindled. Slowly, steadily and surely, they failed to adapt and adjust to new age merchandising, promoting and retail management strategies. They lost their relevancy, their customer base and in 1996...their base business. Woolworth closed its last "five and dime" late in 1997, deep in the shadows of latecomers like Target and Wal-Mart.

They ensured a place in history by being first. They also ensured a place in college business text books as a terrific case study on how to run a once terrific business into the garbage heap. Adieu!

Studebaker, one of the first important American car brands, was established originally as a blacksmith shop just after the Civil War (1866). The company's history spanned nearly a century when a labor dispute that resulted in a long, crippling strike...a rash of quality problems with a number of their car models (i.e., the Lark, the Hawk and the Avanti)...and a series of marketing miscues led Studebaker to its death in 1963.

One of the very first American tire company brands, Goodyear had sixty straight profitable years until 1990, when it suffered a strong market share decline and, uncharacteristically, lost money. Persisting in selling its tires through company-owned stores and independent dealers licensed to sell Goodyear products, consumers saw the Goodyear brand as inconvenient. After all, one could buy Bridgestone, Pirelli, Michelin and a host of other tire brands at warehouse club stores, discount department stores, automotive supply stores and other outlets. In the eyes of consumers, other tire brands were more available than Goodyear. Great companies work to continuously improve, diligently apply lessons learned, and then change. Goodyear made some important changes to get back on track (or back "on road"), the most significant being the expansion of its distribution channels by arranging to sell a number of its tire lines through Sears.

Camel cigarettes was the first branded cigarette in the United States. Up until 1930, when it was surpassed in sales by Lucky Strike (another brand that went from "distinction" to near "extinction"), Camel was also America's number one selling cigarette. In 1964, when the U.S. Surgeon General published the report that claimed "cigarette smoking is a health hazard of sufficient importance in the United States to warrant appropriate remedial action,"[18] Camel sloughed off the report as unimportant to its own future. While its competitors quickly started producing filter-tip cigarettes and making claims of low tar, low nicotine, etc., Camel continued marketing its unadulterated, real taste, real tobacco positioning. Its market share dwindled dramatically and today is more a specialty niche brand than a power player.

The first one in doesn't necessarily cross the finish line first.

There's a lot to be said about the learning derived from the children's story, "The Tortoise and the Hare." First out of the starting blocks did not insure Mr. Hare a victory at the finish line. The consistent, steady, highly focused Mr. Tortoise kept on moving slowly but surely toward his objective and ultimately won the race.

Yes, there are exceptions. Some "first ones in" did, in fact, pass the test of time and successfully remain on top. Every myth certainly has its exceptions.

Coca-Cola was the first one "in." They're still first. Blockbuster Video, Pizza Hut, Yellow Cab, Gillette Safety Razor, Cutex, Vick's Vaporub, Dr. Scholl's Foot Aids, Vaseline Petroleum Jelly, Lea & Perrins Worchester Sauce, Murine Eye Care Products, Philip Morris, Heinz 57, 3M's Scotch Tape, Gold Medal Flour, Life Savers, Wells

Fargo, Morton Salt, Dixie Cup and P&G's Ivory Soap were also first ones "in" and today remain first or near first as category and corporate leaders.

Success is often directly related to having an open mind. Being flexible, agile and adaptive are important business building traits. Sometimes not being first in a particular industry could potentially lead open-minded, agile companies into transferring focus to another industry, a parallel industry or even an emerging industry with even greater success than they had in their original endeavor.

Such was the case with a young, upstart company called The Minnesota Mining and Manufacturing Company, based in Duluth, Minnesota. They were clearly *not* the first company in America to seek its fortune from mining various specialty ores (i.e., corundum, a natural ingredient used in the manufacture of abrasives and sandpaper), but they energetically committed themselves to quality. Transferring focus from mining to manufacturing, they started producing sandpaper under their operating name, The 3M Company. They built their reputation NOT for being first but for being a high-quality producer. In fact, a trade magazine once referred to them as "...a good little maker of sandpaper."

Above and beyond their abrasives and sandpaper business, 3M later entered what proved to be an incredibly lucrative field when they pursued the adhesive tape business. They modeled their product offering after another company's product (probably some now nondescript company that was "first one in"). Initially, they provided masking tape for auto manufacturers to use when they painted two-tone cars to achieve a clean, crisp, sharp edge where one color met the other. Again their products were always considered high-quality and a real value to customers. This reputation for value (called "a bargain" by many) grew rapidly, and eventually one of their accounts referred to 3M's products as "Scotch tape" because it fit a frugal industrial buyer's budget nicely. No pun intended, but the name stuck.

3M then started focusing more effort on what they believed to be an emerging consumer goods market for adhesives. They kept abreast of all sorts of inventions and innovations. In particular, *they closely studied one of the first companies in the business*, observing every move that leader made in the enterprise then referred to as the "pressure sensitive transparent cellophane tape" business. Again, *not* the first one in, 3M improved upon the original processes and products they observed, and came out with their own high-quality adhesive tape, also calling their new tape by the "Scotch" brand name.

The rest is history.

Today there are an astonishing 500-plus varieties of tape bearing the "Scotch" name. Their products are marketed all around the world and they are clearly the category leader. Needless to say, they've come a long, long way from their one room Duluth office adjacent to a specialty ore mine. They've also skyrocketed their reputation from just being a "good little maker of sandpaper" to their current stature and prominent position as a multibillion dollar world class leader.

The first one in doesn't necessarily win. Innovators win. Opportunists win. Best in class wins, and victorious, highly successful 3M became best in class.

Having spent a great deal of time working with (and for) incredibly large, prosperous Australian, British, Canadian and Japanese business clients, I've noticed an interesting phenomenon. Each international executive and development team I've counseled was incredibly interested in spending more time in the field observing businesses than in spending time in a conference room engaged in strategic planning. They were all nearly obsessive about viewing and visiting many U.S. businesses similar to their own in hopes of picking up new ideas, innovative concepts, "best practice" examples, and education.

In fact, one of the most successful consulting services my firm ever provided clients was what we called a "workshop on wheels," a virtual field trip filled with first-hand observation, lots of business visitation and an abundance of "hands on" learning. Simply put, we'd fly into a city, rent a van, pile in client executives and a consulting "guide" and off we'd go into our marvelous classroom on the road.

But here is the challenge to conventional wisdom in all this. When asked about original innovation, business creation and being the "first one in," each of my international guests openly and candidly admitted they had absolutely no reservation about *not* being first in a venture. In fact, they all had a clear inclination toward being second or third with an energetic focus on taking the best of what they saw from "first one in" innovation and improving upon the work back home in their own countries. In particular, one of my Aussie buddies from Sydney boldly laughed and said, "It's simple for us. We study what American and Japanese innovators do, bring it back to Australia and improve upon it. First isn't important. Better is our objective. Call us followers, imitators, call us what you will...but being the best is all we care about, mate! And in the end, 'being best' is what we get called the most."

BEING THE BEST IS ALL WE SHOULD CARE ABOUT

If you analyze the activities, programs, products and initiatives put forth by those "first one in" companies that have succeeded, you'd find that success over the long haul came about because of a solid business foundation, a culture oriented toward adaptation, a clear vision for specific positioning, and an open mind toward repositioning, reinventing and redefining (especially business policies, procedures, standards and practices).

You'd also find that "first one in" companies (and products) that have remained first, over the years, have usually been obsessive about continuous improvement. In short, they viewed their job as never being done. When asked when he thought his dream project, Disneyworld, would be completed, Walt Disney replied, "As long as there is imagination in the world, Disneyworld will NEVER be completed."

Unfortunately, many companies and products that were the "first one in" ended up in a less-than-preferred, often tragic way.

It's real simple. Be the best, the very best you can be in a company, a category and a career and you ensure longevity and lasting success.

Being the best requires a "cut above the rest" mentality. Being the best also requires an aversion to anything that comes close to resembling "me, too."

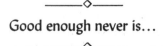

Good enough never is...

———◇———

Celebrate your uniqueness and settle for nothing less than a "best in class" position. And remember, being first is nice, however, exceeding your own expectations and being the best in class is much more important (and lasting).

Being the best is all we should care about, mate!

Challenge the Myths of
Your Own Conventional Wisdom...

CHAPTER HIGHLIGHTS

- "Better" is better than first.
- Furthermore, being "best" is even more important than being first.
- You don't have to be "first" to try harder and excel.
- The first one in the race doesn't necessarily cross the finish line first.
- Success is often directly related to having an open mind. Being flexible, agile and adaptable are important business-building traits. Sometimes not being first in a particular industry could potentially lead open-minded, agile companies into transferring focus to another industry, a parallel industry or even an emerging industry with even greater success than they had previously experienced in their original endeavor.
- The first one in doesn't necessarily win. Innovators win. Opportunists win.
- Being the best is all we should care about.
- Being the best requires a "cut above the rest" mentality. Being the best also requires an aversion to anything that comes close to resembling "me, too."
- Good enough never is...

◇

Myth Seven

BACK TO BASICS

Nothing is absolute.

Even myths have merit.

In other words, phrases used in this book that depict major myths in business, if controlled...if taken in conservative doses...and if managed...may very well represent viable strategies. The problem, however, is that many business people take each phrase literally and blindly block out any alternative or alteration of each stated principle and old rule.

Such is often the case with the "Back-to-Basics" myth.

On the surface, it seems viable. Going back to the basic tenets and guiding principles of one's business such as honesty, integrity, strong work ethic, on time deliveries, rapid customer reaction, etc. have validity. On the other hand, repeating over and over again the unsuccessful patterns of operating style, management culture, marketing position, sales approaches and financial behaviors that may have contributed to the problematic existing state of affairs makes going "back-to-basics" a foolhardy program.

It's all about balance.

When going back to the basics or the roots of a business in hopes of fixing an ailing or slumping enterprise, it is critical to analyze every functional area of the business and take stock in what is important and what is not, what is working and what is not, what are both the assets and deficits of the business model and thoroughly analyze why, unfortunately, the company is under-performing.

For purposes of illustration, I've created a fictitious example of a company that is having trouble with what we'll call "customer response time." Step by step, we will review the issue and through example, show where "back-to-basics" should be viewed as a myth to stay away from, as well as where it might also be a necessary improvement strategy.

Let's pretend that this particular company had received a number of complaints related to its customer response system. The following represents a list of non-negotiable service levels, you know, "basics" of this company's customer response program:

- Every incoming telephone call will be answered by a person, not an automatic voicemail transfer system.

- Every telephone ring will be answered, ideally, on the first ring and certainly by the second ring.

- Every salutation will be energetic, upbeat and positive.

- Every incoming telephone call will be quickly directed to the proper department. If a department line is busy, however, the caller will be given the option of either holding on the line for an available representative or going into the representative's voice mailbox.

- Every customer order will be processed immediately. There is nothing more important than incoming orders. Orders will *not* sit on a desk while "other" activities are accomplished, nor will they be left in a holding tray while a representative takes a break. They will be processed immediately.

- Every order received will immediately be followed by a hearty "thank you " from the order taker over the phone and a fax (or e-mail) confirmation of the order will be sent within three hours of each order received.

Again, this fictitious short list of customer response principles was designed to provide an illustration of "what's important" for this example company to provide the right response for each customer. If we were analyzing *every* aspect of this business, aggressively and desperately seeking to find gaps in the operation, we would likely take this list and review each functional step in the process, seeing whether or not the company was fulfilling its principles. In other words, were the phones being answered on the first or second ring? Were orders being immediately processed? Etcetera.

If not, this would be a time to go "back-to-basics" if we were still convinced that the basics were viable, meaningful and realistic.

Let's, for example sake, put forth the following observations and findings to further our case study with this fictitious company.

- The incoming switchboard and one-person operation is incapable of personally answering each incoming call, especially on the first or second ring.

- The steady flow of incoming orders, especially at peak periods, prevent the order takers from processing orders until there's a lull in order-placing calls. If the order takers process orders directly upon receiving them, other incoming calls will have to go into voicemail and likely not receive "call backs" for long periods of time.

- Immediately sending a fax or e-mail was time-consuming and dramatically cut into order-receiving and processing activity time.

Not to belabor the point, however, if the above observations were valid, our management conclusions would likely be these:

- Our customer response principles are important and valid. Let's not change our "basic" principles. They are sound.

- We don't have the proper technological nor human resources to effectively execute against those principles. We have gaps.

Therefore, going "back-to-basics" in ideology, theory and principle is right on target, however, if all we do is push back "to basics" without making some major operational changes, we won't improve our operation.

And so, simply mandating and directing employees to go back to the basic principles of customer response service would be ludicrous. They would likely agree with the prescription but nonetheless are incapable of implementing the process.

Now would be the time to balance "back-to-basics."

The "basic" fundamental philosophies and doctrines of operation are perfectly suited for the business at hand, however, the "basic" programs, processes and systems to fulfill those tenets of operation are outdated, irrelevant and poorly managed.

Is "back-to-basics," then, a myth? Is "back-to-basics," then, a viable business development strategy? Yes and yes! Back-to-basics, in philosophy and *ideology*, is "usually" an on-target position. However, back-to-basics in operation*s* is usually off target because of ineffective, unproductive and antiquated systems.

Logically, when a company is ailing or even failing, pushing back to the way its always done things may be a devastatingly bad remedy. After all, it's very likely that the reason an enterprise is in the jam it's in is because of the way its always operated. Back-to-basics, then, could prove even more destructive.

The key message is a simple one. Keep those behavior basics that work and trash those basics that no longer work.

In other words, do the right thing.

I've often thought that part of a company's business plan should be chiseled out in stone (i.e., vision, mission, guiding principles) while other parts of the plan should be scratched out in pencil (i.e., objectives, strategies, tactics, targets, etc.). The stone engraved plan elements are forever...are non-negotiables. On the other hand, the pencil etchings are fluid, flexible and should move with the times.

Thus, the back-to-basics theory works with the rock solid, mandatory stone carved precepts, yet, constantly changes with the ever-erasable pencil parts.

———◇———

There's the difference. Going back to the basics of "WHAT" we do, such as provide high-quality products should be cast in stone. Going back to the basics of "HOW" we do it can change over and over again and should be inscribed in pencil.

———◇———

PRINCIPLES TO CHISEL IN STONE

Here are ten examples of the kinds of principles that should be chiseled in stone. These "back-to-basics" (the "what") shouldn't be altered.

- Sell solutions, not just products.
- Offer the customer something unique and special.
- Provide the customer additional reasons to buy from us.
- Never forget that the customer is the very reason we're in business.
- Constantly implement new, improved, convenient service systems.
- Work to receive both customer feedback and employee ideas and input.

- Provide products for different types of customers and their need states.
- Diligently dedicate resources toward continuous improvement.
- Provide a high level of value and focused efforts directed toward customer satisfaction.
- Make doing business with us easy, special, unique and always positive.

In turn, here are ten examples of the kinds of programs that could be scratched out in pencil, all capable of being changed. In other words, these "back-to-basics" (the "how") should be regularly reviewed and altered if applicable and appropriate.

- Develop all trade advertising and public relations through our very own in-house creative agency.
- Sell our products and services through a highly developed broker and independent representative network.
- Outsource many of our integral production components to international producers.
- Distribute our merchandise through a DSD (direct store delivery) system on our own transportation vehicles.
- Require that all director level personnel work out of the home office.
- Never strategically align or cooperatively market our goods and services with another company.
- Develop our own in-house field quality management team and infrastructure.
- Avoid allocating resources directed toward trade association activities.
- Provide bracket pricing, volume discounts and special terms for larger customers.
- Protect our brand and never enter into a co-pack or private label relationship program.

———◇———

"Back-to-basics," therefore, is situational, issue-related and
either relevant or irrelevant, predicated on whether we're
talking about standards and guiding principles ("what" we do)
or procedures, policies and practices ("how" we do it).

———◇———

I admire Tyson Foods, the U.S. national leader in poultry processing. They're energetic, innovative, customer-focused and highly successful.

In the early 1970s, I had the opportunity to sit in on a meeting that included Don Tyson, Tyson Foods' founder and chairman, and some key executives from the Southland Corporation (7-11 Convenience Stores). 7-11 had an interest in purchasing a specific Tyson fully-cooked, microwavable product, however, was concerned that the carton pack size was much too large for both the small freezer space available in each 7-11 store and the projected customer sales for the product.

A 7-11 executive asked Don Tyson, "Why do you pack these products ninety-six units to the case? Our available freezers are much too small to stock the product...plus, it might take us a number of weeks to sell a case. They're too large." Tyson's response perfectly exemplified the dichotomy of "back to basic" viewpoints.

His first reply was something to the effect of, "We're here for you. If ninety-six units to the case isn't meaningful, we'll figure out a way to change the pack so we can do business with you. We'll provide you a pack size that makes the most sense for your operation."

That's an example of a chiseled-in-stone "back-to-basic" Tyson guiding principle that clearly says Tyson is a customer-focused company that will adapt, adjust and alter products, programs and in this case, packaging, specifically for important customers. Don't change this "basic," Don.

Mr. Tyson continued, "As to why we pack these products ninety-six to the case, I'm not sure of the answer. However, I'll get back to you on it. Again, however, the most important message here is that we'll work with you. What size pack do you think would work best?"

This second response represents the "in pencil" positioning that says "how" Tyson services its customers can, in fact, be altered. Make some "basic" changes here, Mr. Tyson. Go for it, get the order!

As it turned out, the reason Tyson Foods packed this particular product 96 units to the case was simple. It was the way it had always been done. In reality, years before, some corrugated box salesman sold Tyson a standard-sized carton which nicely held 96 pieces. Clearly, that wasn't a "basic" worth debating. Tyson emphasized its "basic" guiding principle of customer flexibility by altering the "basic" way it packed a product for 7-11 and obviously, Tyson got the order.

The basic marketing position and phrase Hallmark Cards has used for decades is "Hallmark Cards...when you care enough to send the very best!"

That "basic" will likely never change, however, over the years, although Hallmark's words have been consistent, many of the ancillary creative elements surrounding the phrase have changed. For instance, the font used in various advertisements has changed, the colors used in marketing materials has changed, the musical background styles in commercials has changed...all to fit the media, consumer targets and times.

Again, it's the basic "what" ("What" does Hallmark stand for?) that remains constant while the basics of "how" ("How" does Hallmark convey what it stands for?) stays flexible.

More of the same can be good.

More of the same can also be bad.

———◇———

Blend a little "what" with lots of alternative "hows" and an enterprise will ultimately establish a viable positioning for addressing the "basics."

———◇———

Going back to the basics of traditional Disney marketing and management proved to be disastrous for its Euro-Disney property. The European culture, business climate and economy drastically differed from the U.S. and required an entirely different approach to business building. Details are presented in "Myth 9—Close Enough Is Good Enough" in this book. The key to remember here, however, is that a "back-to-basics" approach in an entirely new market environment will likely not work.

By the same token, when Sears started experiencing dramatic sales declines from their history-making catalogue (established in 1896), they made the wrong decision to "go back-to-basics" and aggressively continue marketing the publication the way it had always been marketed. Instead of, perhaps, learning from what had been called catalogue "browsing books," such as Land's End, J. Crew, Tweeds, Talbots, L.L. Bean, Victoria's Secret and other successes...Sears kept on pushing the "same old" strategies and tactics. By not changing, by being inflexible, by taking an aggressive "back-to-basics" approach, by not adapting to consumer lifestyle changes (i.e., women in the work force, interest in online shopping, electronic commerce, etc.)...Sears continued to fail and ultimately closed its catalogue division in 1993.

Not seeing consumers shift from "dieting" to eating "healthy," Heinz saw its Weight Watchers diet-positioned brand drop over $100-million in sales from 1990-1993. Instead of aggressively altering their plans and positioning, Weight Watchers kept focusing on the "basic" precepts and marketing premises that worked in years past. Big mistake! While Weight Watchers pushed "back-to-basics," Nestle's Lean Cuisine, Con Agra's Healthy Choice and Le Menu from the Campbell Soup Company all moved forward and provided the consumer "new" healthful alternatives to Weight Watchers products and conversely, grabbed share from Heinz.

Again, it's important to restate that "back-to-basics" can be a double-edge sword. On one hand, going back to the basic tenets and guiding principles of a business (the "what") may be a viable, important strategy. However, when things are ailing or failing, moving away from the "basic" operational aspects of the business (the "how") makes good sense.

Sitting on a panel at a conference with Bill Marriott, I remember a wonderful "back-to-basics" story he shared with the audience.

When his father, J. Willard Marriott, Sr., the Chairman and CEO of the Marriott Corporation, decided to retire and name his son Bill as successor, he called Bill into his office and told him to start preparing a "state of the company" address to be delivered to all the key Marriott executives from around the world at an upcoming meeting. Needless to say, the meeting took on an incredible degree of importance for young Bill in lieu of the fact that it would be his very first corporate address in his new role as Marriott president.

He turned to his father for advice and asked, "Dad, I want to make sure my speech is perfect and provides our key executives the right kind of message and leadership. Do you have any suggestions?"

The senior Marriott looked his son squarely in the eyes and said, "Tell them not to cook the pancakes in advance of orders. They dry out on the grill and taste terrible."

Young Bill Marriott was astonished. He responded, "Dad, this is my first corporate address as President. I can't talk to these key executives about pancakes. I need something stronger. Seriously, got any ideas?"

Mr. Marriott again responded to his son, this time with a more serious tone, and sternly said, "Bill, there is absolutely nothing...nothing more important you can tell our people than not to allow the pancakes to be cooked in advance. Bill, they dry out on the grill and taste absolutely terrible. Take that message to the meeting. It's very important!"

Bill Marriott eventually realized the importance of his father's advice. The learning is obvious. An important Marriott guiding principle is guest satisfaction through quality products. J.W. Marriott was right. There was nothing more important than conveying to the group how critical it must be for Marriott to maintain its high quality standards.

That surely was a "back-to-basic" tenet worth restating, revisiting and reinforcing. It represented the "what" of Marriott's business and should be held sacred. "Back-to-basics" related to the "how" of a business can be kept or discarded depending on whether it's still viable.

Don't cook the pancakes in advance. They dry out on the grill and taste terrible.

Challenge the Myths of Your Own Conventional Wisdom...

CHAPTER HIGHLIGHTS
- Nothing is absolute. Even myths have merit. Such is often the case with the "back-to-basics" myth.

- Going back to the basic tenets and guiding principles of one's business such as honesty, integrity, strong work ethic, on time deliveries, rapid customer reaction, etc. all have validity. On the other hand, repeating over and over again the same "basic" unsuccessful patterns of operating style, management culture, marketing position, sales approaches and financial behaviors that may have contributed to the problematic existing state of affairs makes going "back-to-basics" a foolhardy program.

- When going back to the basics or the roots of a business in hopes of fixing an ailing or slumping enterprise, it is critical to analyze every functional area of the business and take stock in what is important and what is not, what is working and what is not, what are both the assets and deficits of the business model and thoroughly analyze why, unfortunately, the company is under-performing.

- Oftentimes, the "basic" fundamental philosophies and doctrines of operation are perfectly suited for the business at hand, however, the "basic" programs, processes and systems to fulfill those tenets of operation are outdated, irrelevant and poorly managed.

- Back-to-basics, in philosophy and ideology, is "usually" an on target position.

- Back-to-basics, in operations, on the other hand, may be off target because of ineffective, unproductive and antiquated systems.

- Back-to-basics, therefore, is situational, issue-related and either relevant or irrelevant predicated upon whether we're talking about standards and guiding principles ("what" we do) or procedures, policies and practices ("how" we do it).

- This is one of the times when "more of the same" (back-to-basics) can be good. Needless to say, we already know that "more of the same" can also be bad.

- Blend a little "what" with lots of alternative "hows" and an enterprise can ultimately establish a viable positioning for addressing the "basics."

◇

MYTH EIGHT

BUSINESS IS COMPLEX

I've heard it said over and over again, "Business is complex. Business success isn't easy. Operating a business is difficult." I regularly respond to these statements with a bold, "NOT!"

We make business complicated by poor (or no) plans and planning, by ineffectual execution, by bad staffing decisions and by faulty positioning.

I, for one, believe business can be a relatively simple, one dimensional thing.

———◇———

**There are only two basic activities in business—
selling and supporting the selling.**

———◇———

If you're the chairman of the board, your role and primary activity is to "support the selling." You should be gathering resources, hiring thoroughbred leaders, building factories, funding technical services and developing sales incentives designed to drive the sales effort and "support the selling."

Whether you're a receptionist, loading dock foreman, secretary, head of human resources, manufacturing director or controller...you're primary activity is to support the selling.

———◇———

NOTHING, absolutely nothing happens until something is sold.

———◇———

Sales represents the engine that drives the company vehicle.

It's almost funny...ludicrous...when you consider how companies that suffer financial and other business troubles seem to be inclined to cut their sales force as opposed to paring down other functional areas. Cutting a sales force is like cutting a jugular vein. The result...death to the body, death to the company.

Peter Drucker also believes in the simplicity of business as well. He said, "Business has only two basic functions...marketing and innovation."

Anyway you slice the cake, business shouldn't be viewed as complex.

Sure, one could draw a good case for the complexities of various specific business functions. Cost accounting can be challenging. Product development can be arduous. Distribution and logistics can be difficult. Quality management can be a drudgery.

But that goes, as they say, "with the territory."

In the early years of the TV comedy show "Saturday Night Live,"[19] in 1978, there was a regular onscreen character who portrayed a cerebral, philosophical priest, Father Guido Sarducci (played by comedian Don Novello). I found one of his skits (later to appear on an album, cassette tape and CD) particularly funny and memorable.

The skit (or "bit") Father Sarducci presented was called "The Five-Minute University."

His contention was that everything we learned in college could have been compressed, delivered and effectively presented by a savvy professor in a focused five minutes—as opposed to four-plus long, drawn-out years.

Particularly meaningful to the messages in this chapter were the following business administration courses described by the good Father who asserted that key business postulates were actually very simple. For example, a course in Business, paraphrased, went something like this:

"Okay class. It's time for BUSINESS 101. It's really very simple. It's a three-word class: '*Make a profit!*' That's it. Class dismissed!"

He continued (and I paraphrase)....

"Let's move on to ECONOMICS. Are you ready? Two words are all you need to know: '*supply and demand.*' That's the course. Take a break!"

And what about "SALES," "PURCHASING" and "MARKET-ING?"

"Welcome to our ten-second class in SALES. Pencils ready? *Get the order....get the order!* Go stretch and get ready for the next module."

"As to the key to successful PURCHASING. Here's the class: *Buy cheap!*"

"It's time for INTRODUCTION TO MARKETING. 'Find a need and fill it. If there's no need, create one!' School's out."

According to Father Sarducci, a key word or phrase is all one needs to know to define a discipline.

Sure, five minutes to a university degree is a bit silly (I believe twenty minutes is far more realistic), however, in his unique comedic way, Father Guido supported my point that business is very simple. We complicate it by overthinking and underacting.

The irony is that Guido's advice to "Make a profit" probably is all one should be focusing on when building a business and it certainly shouldn't take an entire semester to learn it. Without profit, you're out of business. Sarducci's simplified viewpoint, ironically enough, is similar to that of world-class capitalist and entrepreneur Bernard Baruch who, when asked by a young man if there was a sure way to make a million dollars in business, responded, "All you need to do is purchase a million bags of flour at one dollar and sell them for two dollars each."

Business is, in fact, simple. Make a profit!

———◇———

We work diligently to make business more and more complicated. That's all some people ever talk about.

———◇———

I guess if they didn't fill their conversations with chatter about how difficult their business lives and specific jobs were then they'd likely devalue their lot in life (and business). It's as if they had a desperate need to justify an existence, job and position by way of bemoaning the tragic fate of being underpaid, overworked and perhaps even underloved.

Nobody ever said it would be easy. Perhaps being strapped with an ever-changing, ever-challenging, ever-difficult business life is par for the course. Maybe, as the title of the wonderful Jack Nicholson movie reads, this is "As Good As It Gets."

Sure, there are challenges.

After all, company after company that missed, or failed completely for that matter, overlooked many simple truths of business.

Union Pacific Railroad established a terrible reputation. Instead of becoming known for quality service, consistent customer satisfaction and "on time" deliveries...they were known, instead, for aggravating customers, damaging freight, having inflexible schedules, constantly incurring shipping delays and suffering from an abundance of equipment failures.

Business isn't complex. A positive reputation is critical. Union Pacific forgot a simple truth...the customer comes first. That's simple stuff!

Avon Products forgot how important adapting and adjusting to consumer demographic changes are in keeping a business vibrant and viable. Their traditional door-to-door campaign was no longer relevant (Ding, dong! "Avon calling!") in a mid-1990s America that saw a huge number of women working outside the home. In short, women were no longer at home when Avon came "calling." Also, consumer concerns of safety and security made "cold calling" on a door-to-door basis an unrealistic selling strategy. After all, a 1990s consumer is reluctant to answer a doorbell from a stranger. Highly secured apartments and condominiums have security guards, doors with electronic lock releases, closed circuit televisions and rules for allowing strangers to enter a building, etc.

Business isn't complex. It's simple. Change with the times. Perhaps marketing to women in the workplace, using online ordering services or engaging in mail order would be more meaningful for Avon.

In March 1985, "New Coke" was a dismal, highly-publicized failure. Business Week called the fiasco "the marketing blunder of the decade." In short, although consumers did like "New Coke's taste, they were enraged to learn that it would completely replace Coke's "classic" version. Coca-Cola headquarters received over 8,000 telephone calls a day in outrage and 40,000 letters a day in protest. When Coca-Cola changed direction and announced the re-introduction of Coke "Classic" television programming all around the United States interrupted their broadcasts to provide viewers a special bulletin. Senator David Pryor of Arkansas openly expressed his excited approval of the move while addressing the U.S. Senate. New Coke lost its fizz.

Business isn't complex. Don't mess with a trusted brand. Create line extensions, new package forms, new ingredient formulations for different consumer groups, even a new graphics and design look, however, don't take the leader (of leaders in this case) and claim there's a better brand flavor profile in the portfolio. Anything less than a "classic" could never be "the real thing!"

Business isn't complex. Required adjustments and solutions are usually simpler than we assume.

Most solutions come from simple, workable, realistic approaches to problem-solving. Move a machine two feet that way, hire a new sales rep for an emerging market, develop a line extension for a mature market, refuse to sell a constantly delinquent customer, backhaul products on a trucking route for logistical efficiency, study "best practices" in employee motivation and on and on and on.

Business is *not* complicated "if" companies and executives focus on logical approaches to growth. We overthink, overreact and overcomplicate and for whatever reason, we ignore logic.

Academy Award winning actor, Spencer Tracy, was interviewed by a reporter who asked, "Mr. Tracy, acting seems very difficult and complex. What do you think makes for accomplished acting?" Tracy responded, "It's simple. Know your lines and don't bump into furniture."

Yes, it's simple. Don't bump into the furniture!

———◇———

The key to keeping business manageable and relatively
uncomplicated is education.

———◇———

With the incredible opportunities we have today to continue learning, I am convinced the companies that will win in the future will *not* be the "learned" but the "learning!" It's an ongoing process that keeps a company fresh, vibrant, innovative and positioned as a leader.

BUSINESS SIMPLIFIED

How does one simplify a business?

It all starts with the game "mirror, mirror on the wall."

Before a business can be less complex and certainly before any significant business building takes place, a company MUST answer the following questions simply, succinctly and honestly.

- Who are we?
- What do we stand for?
- Why are we here? Why do we exist?
- What are we committed to provide?
- What are our guiding principles?
- What is our purpose?
- What is our short- and long-term vision?
- What is our specific mission?
- How do (and will) we define success?

If anything, technology has given us the opportunity to simplify both our businesses and our lives.

Consider that businesses of old were obsessively focused on complex products ("things"). Yes, "things" like oil (Rockefeller), steel (Carnegie), ships (Getty), plastics (DuPont) and cars (Ford) were the basis of huge industries and businesses...and each created incredible wealth for their leader innovators. Today, however, it's actually simpler. Apple, Dell, Intel, IBM, Microsoft and others base their entire businesses on "intangibles" like ideas, information, access and solutions.

At his business peak, nearing seventy years of age, oilman John D. Rockefeller (1839-1937) was personally worth about $12 billion. In 1997, Microsoft's founder and chairman, 42-year-old Bill Gates, built his personal wealth to an excess of $42 billion...and it all came from ideas, information and access...NOT tangible hard goods and products.

Sure, skeptics cry "foul" and claim that inflation might have made Rockefeller's fortune comparable to Gates'. However, if you factor in variances for inflation, on a similar scale, Rockefeller would have been worth approximately $29 billion at age 69 to Gates' $42 billion at age 42. Gates is still the winner! Oh by the way, as of 1997, Gates was still growing his net worth and fortune.

There was only so much oil that could be pulled from the ground and pumped into metal drums. On the other hand, there is no end to the ideas, information, access and solutions companies like Microsoft can provide its global customers.

Packaging, distribution and logistics have "simply" been on Bill Gates' side. The fact of the matter is that packaging, distribution, logistics and a barrel full of other business activities are "simply" on the side of every company that deals in ideas, information, access and solutions.

————◇————

We are our own worst enemies.
We make business complicated.

————◇————

Consider, for instance, that many companies employ people who carry the word "research" someplace in their titles and on their fancy embossed business cards, yet, these same corporations still slam tons of resources against "outsourced" white papers, data dumps, gap analysis, examinations and studies. Why even have a research department if most of the data comes from outside research companies?

————◇————

Study this….study that….it's the American way. We make our
businesses complex by propagating a culture of "analysis paralysis"
that keeps us reading and reviewing data in lieu of and in place of
acting, doing and executing.

————◇————

A simpler way to grow forward is to glean "just enough" data to justify an initiative and then take it to the streets. How's this for a simple strategy?

- Produce it.
- Test it.
- Refine it.
- Sell the hell out of it!

Sounds simple, doesn't it? I especially like the well-directed notion that once a product or program is "refined," simply "sell the hell out of it!" That's productive stuff!

Speaking of "productive stuff," I either heard or read a viewpoint that the concept of productivity was basically very simple. The author conveyed his point by using the example of professional baseball players and their batting records. The analogy went something to the effect of...

A pro baseball player who gets one hit every four times at bat achieves a .250 batting average and probably earns a few hundred thousand dollars in salary. He is considered a marginal hitter. On the other hand, a player who gets one hit in every three times at bat achieves a .333 batting average, is considered a superstar and likely earns a few million dollars in salary. Since most players get to bat four times in a game, all a player has to do is get one additional hit (above his one-in-four average) in twelve times at bat to go from .250 to .333...and be considered a star...and earn the big bucks.

It all boils down to the fact that the difference between "ordinary" and "EXTRAordinary" is just a little "extra."

Want to understand how much productivity is needed to accomplish a specific target? No sweat! Break down the objectives sought into bite-size, easy-to-understand, easy-to-communicate pieces and the task at hand, as well as the challenge, will be dimensionalized, quantified, and simplified.

Simplicity is smart.

We have "smart cards" for financial simplicity. Why not "smart processes" for business simplicity?

You see "simple" comes from planning your work and working your plan. Without a well-organized portfolio of plans, business will be complex.

Want to simplify the business and avoid unnecessary "dead end streets," wrong turns and wasted travel time en route to accomplishing objectives and business building? Create a road map. Yes, simplify the process by creating, developing and implementing a "business plan," a "marketing plan," a "long-range plan," a "contingency plan" and perhaps even a "quantum leap big idea plan."

Before the planning should commence, however, businesses need to clearly understand where they are and where they ideally want to be going.

Lewis Carroll's lines from *Alice In Wonderland*[20] describe this nicely.

"Chesire-puss," she began, rather timidly..."would you tell me which way I ought to go from here?"

"That depends a good deal on where you want to get to," said the cat.

"I don't much care where..." said Alice.

"Then it doesn't matter which way you go," said the cat.

It truly doesn't matter which way you go if you don't care where you ultimately want to arrive. You've got to have a well-defined destination in mind for business planning to work. Also, there's absolutely no reason why that destination can't be a stretch, can't be high.

Fail to plan? Plan to fail!

Henry David Thoreau wrote, "In the long run, men only hit what they aim at. Therefore, though they should fail immediately, they had better aim at something high."

Here's an easy business plan template that's always worked for me and my world class clients:

- *Situation Analysis*—Snapshots of the economy, industry, competitive sets, business opportunities, etc.
- *Vision*—Long-term, why does the company exist? What does the company hope to become? In a macro sense, where are you going?
- *Mission*—Shorter-term, where are you heading? What is the primary task at hand?

- *Objectives*—What do you hope to accomplish in a finite period of time? How will it be measured? What does success look like?

- *Barriers to Achieving Objectives*—What might get in the way? What should you be prepared for that might be an impediment to success?

- *Strategies*—What are the ways you'll achieve the objectives set?

- *Guiding Principles*—What do you stand for? What will you do and what won't you do in your quest for achieving stated objectives?

- *Tactics*—What are the specific step-by-step, point-by-point activities and initiatives you'll implement to support the mission, objectives and strategies.

- *Timeline*—What is the specific calendar "action line" that defines the achievement process?

- *Targets*—What are your business development targets and why?

- *Budget*—What is the resource allocation? How much will you spend to achieve your objectives?

- *Implementation and Control*—How will you measure and track all activities on the road to success?

- *Supporting Material, Resources and References*—This is a compilation of the most important readings, research, resources and references that accompany your plan, campaign and specific initiatives...and support both the premises and plan.

Even the decision-making process in business is often unduly overcomplicated. One simplification formula for decision-making worth noting is referred to as "The ABCs Of Decision-Making."

A. Analyze the alternatives.

B. Balance the benefits of each alternative.

C. Calculate the contingencies (How can each alternative help us? How can each alternative hurt us?).

D. Decide! Make a decision.

E. Execute!

Business can be simple if we apply logical approaches to the opportunities and issues.

Hey, Guido...thanks a lot for the insight.

Hey, readers...it's simple. *Make a profit!*

Challenge the Myths of Your Own Conventional Wisdom...

CHAPTER HIGHLIGHTS

- We make business complicated by poor (or no) plans and planning, by ineffectual execution, by bad staffing decisions and by faulty positioning.
- There are only two basic activities in business. Selling and supporting the selling.
- Nothing, absolutely nothing happens until something is sold.
- We work diligently to make business more and more complicated. That's all some people ever talk about.
- We over-think, overreact and overcomplicate and for whatever reason, we ignore logic.
- The key to keeping business manageable and relatively uncomplicated is education.
- Before a business can become less complex and certainly before any significant business building takes place, a company *must* answer the following questions simply, succinctly and honestly.
  - ◇ Who are we?
  - ◇ What do we stand for?
  - ◇ Why are we here? Why do we exist?
  - ◇ What are we committed to provide?
  - ◇ What are our guiding principles?
  - ◇ What is our purpose?
  - ◇ What is our short- and long-term vision?
  - ◇ What is our specific mission?
  - ◇ How do (and will) we define success?
- We are our own worst enemies. We make business complicated.

- Study this...study that...it's the American way. We make our businesses complex by propagating a culture of "analysis paralysis" that keeps us reading and reviewing data in lieu of and in place of acting, doing and executing.
- Here's a much simpler strategy.
  - ◇ Produce it.
  - ◇ Test it.
  - ◇ Refine it.
  - ◇ Sell the hell out of it!
- The difference between "ordinary" and "EXTRAordinary" is just a little "extra."
- Simplicity is smart. We have "smart cards" for financial simplicity. Why not "smart processes" for business simplicity?
- "Simplicity" comes from planning your work and working your plan.
- The ABCs Of Decision Making:
  A. Analyze the alternatives.
  B. Balance the benefits.
  C. Calculate the contingencies.
  D. Decide! Make a decision.
  E. Execute!

◇

MYTH NINE

CLOSE ENOUGH IS GOOD ENOUGH

Cave men scraped and scratched pictures and symbols on rock with their blunt, primitive fist hatchets. Egyptian scribes carved their hieroglyphics with sharp chisels. American colonialists had their quill pens, school children in the middle 1900s had their inkwell feather pens; then came fine point ink cartridge pens, reliable ball point pens, laser point pens, etc. Why the parade of better writing instruments? Simply put, everyone who has ever inscribed or written anything has wanted to convey a cleaner, crisper, sharper image. Close enough has never been good enough.

We've gone from manual typewriters to electric typewriters, from dot matrix printers to laser jet printers, from surface missiles to "smart bombs," and more.

Historically, man has always endeavored for higher, faster, better and, of course, closer.

———◇———

In our high-tech age of exactness, preciseness,
correctness and absolute "on-the-money-ness"
...close enough is *not* good enough.

———◇———

If the 1991 Persian Gulf War taught the world anything, it should have educated and introduced us all to new age air warfare via a laser-driven weapon called the "smart bomb." Created for perfection, "close" was not its objective.

Shotguns come close to hitting a target, a rifle comes even closer, but the "smart bomb" is always a perfect, direct hit.

In an age of absolute technological preciseness, "smart bomb marketing" is the only acceptable initiative. If it's not a "direct hit" today, it's *not* a hit!

As America's love affair with weight control, nutrition and fitness grew in the early 1970s, many companies and new products designed to capitalize on a more health-conscious consumer emerged. Most are gone simply because they got "close" with their products, programs and offerings....but didn't hit the mark squarely enough to achieve long-lasting success.

"Thin's In," "Weigh In," "Nature's Weigh," "LoCal," "NoCal," "Shape Up," "Right Weigh" and a host of other manufacturers came out of the shoot with promises of products and services all designed to help America eat healthy and feel good.

Where are they now?

Some are still niche players on remote grocery and specialty store shelves. Some are gone completely and are only remembered by old-timers like me. Still, the hopes that have long been forgotten and the aspirations that have escaped each of those entrepreneurs makes for many sad stories.

They had what seemed to be the *right idea.* They got close—very close.

Yet, somewhere between the right idea and being close, they fell short of their mark—for a myriad of reasons.

Many of the products tasted awful, vile for that matter. Yes, although they persuaded many consumers that the products were good for their bodies, they also convinced consumers that "good-for-you food" probably had to taste bad to be effective. The odors were terrible. The eye appeal on many of the products was unacceptable. Since many of the products didn't seem designed for human consumption, nobody bought the products and manufacturer after manufacturer shuttered their doors.

Packaging and positioning was also a problem. The last thing a chubby person wanted to see boldly depicted on a package of food was another chubby person. Some consumers believed the packaging was insulting and degrading. The package design, graphics, visuals, etc. turned more consumers off than on.

Product flavors went from bland to blander. There was little excitement in the product offerings and each of these small companies were much too undercapitalized to support any significant R&D, marketing or promotional efforts.

They were all "close" by attacking what was obviously a marketplace opportunity—but "close" was not a match. It wasn't enough. They failed miserably.

Obviously learning from predecessors' past mistakes, companies like Weight Watchers, Lean Cuisine and Healthy Choice used a more focused, laser approach to capitalizing on the health, fitness and "better-for-you" food market opportunities. Their products tasted great, were attractively packaged, energetically marketed and supported by dynamic advertising—providing their customers with convenient, flavorful, trendy offerings...they each enjoyed great success.

It's not surprising that Heinz (Weight Watchers), Stouffer's (Lean Cuisine) and Con Agra (Healthy Choice) have all profited by their "Smart Bomb," absolutely on-the-money marketing programs targeted at the healthy food category. Each brand has been a "direct hit" with retailers and consumers alike. "Close enough" was never their objective.

Everyone, every company makes mistakes.

Disney is no exception.

However, just as it would be difficult to find a more successful, beloved, terrifically successful enterprise than Disney, it is also difficult to find a better example of a startling and surprising failure than its Euro-Disney venture. It's important to note, however, that great companies adapt, adjust and react to challenges. Disney, being a "great company," has corrected many of its early Euro-Disney errors and likely (and logically in the true Disney tradition) will turn around what started out as an ailing enterprise into a hugely successful business endeavor.

"Close enough is *not* good enough" when you're attempting to duplicate or emulate the world's most treasured and successful recreation enterprise (and empire).

It seemed to Disney that building a European Disneyworld was both logical and viable....especially if they built the property *closely* resembling its other successful parks (i.e., Disneyland, Epcot, etc.) and *closely* simulating its proven and successful operating models.

As closely as they tried to duplicate the North American Disney prototypes, it didn't work in Paris. "Close enough" didn't cut it.

Faulty assumptions and false logic led to an ailing and near-failing enterprise, certainly an unusual circumstance for any Disney venture.

Here are some snapshots for review.

Opening in April 1992, the Disney organization was optimistic about Euro-Disney, basing their positive attitude on their huge successes in California, Florida and Japan. The Euro-Disney operation was to *closely* resemble its other properties. Perhaps it was this positioning of "close" that proved problematic in that there were huge cultural differences in theme park patronage in Europe compared to the U.S. Those differences were anything but "close."

Considering that nearly three million guests from Europe visited Disney's U.S. attractions each year, Disney felt comfortable with their forecast of eleven million visitors to Euro-Disney its first year of operation. Although attendance projections were on target with just under one million Euro-Disney visitors a month in 1992, revenues were very flat compared to similar guest-per-capita spending at Disneyland and Disneyworld.

That's where "close enough..." comes into play.

Consumer purchasing patterns in Europe and the United States proved very dissimilar. The patterns weren't even "close."

For instance, in the United States, the average Disney park stay was four days and three nights, while at Euro-Disney, the average stay was two days and one night. Not close! Many U.S. guests either drive great distances to Disneyland or Disneyworld, or fly into California or Florida. Euro-Disney, on the other hand, had many visitors who simply drove two-four hours to visit the park and returned home after the visit.

Due to economic differences between Europe and the U.S., and in part due to France's 1992 recession, guests visiting Euro-Disney were very frugal. For example, many visitors brought their own food into Euro-Disney, an activity rarely seen at Disneyland or Disneyworld. Visitors were also not buying Disney merchandise at a rate anywhere "close" to Disney's other properties. With concession and merchandise sales vital to the financial health of any amusement park, Euro-Disney obviously suffered.

Park admission at Euro-Disney wasn't "close" to the admission price in the U.S. At $42.25 for adults, it was an expensive ticket to buy.

Comparable, in price, to some of the finest hotels in downtown Paris, Euro-Disney hotels suffered from a very low occupancy rate of about sixty percent. The fact that the park was so close and accessible to Paris, many guests simply preferred staying in the heart of downtown instead of adjacent to the amusement park, for the same money. The accessibility of Paris, coupled with the recession (and a downturn in the real estate market), also made it nearly impossible for Disney to sell significant parcels of hotel real estate around the park.

If one just compared this hotel scenario with the Orlando scene where there are "no vacancy" signs on hotel after hotel after hotel...it's obvious that the situations weren't even "close."

Needless to say, there were other problems, as well.

The park initially opened up without serving wine. In a culture where drinking wine with lunch and dinner was acceptable and standard fare, this proved to be a problem (which was later rectified). Disney also miscalculated the demand for breakfast and didn't provide enough breakfast stations for its customers. Allegedly, there were also insufficient bathroom facilities. Etcetera.

Underestimating the dramatic attendance swings they were to have at Euro-Disney and being locked into France's tight employment laws, Disney was also unable to shift employees around to compensate for varying attendance traffic patterns. Hiring was easy, firing was nearly impossible. Disney also learned that training, managing and motivating their Euro-Disney employees was difficult and incredibly different than in Anaheim and Orlando. Attitude, work ethic, respect given management, etc. were all very much different in France.

In 1993, at the end of twenty months of Euro-Disney operations, the park had lost $960 million.

So many of Euro-Disney's initiatives and programs closely resembled its successful U.S. operations. The facilities, the characters, the events, the overall positioning were classic Disney. However, they didn't get "close enough" to the French, much less the European, culture to be successful. In the case of this 5,000-acre, $4.4 billion investment, "close enough was surely *not* good enough."

Investments of this magnitude *require* an absolute "spot on" perfect direct hit. Period!

Initially, Disney executives considered closing the park, however, they decided, instead, to diligently work to improve operations (Disney is famous for its focus on continuous improvement). By 1998, they had already shown a resurgence in profitability and it is my belief that this property, like other Disney properties, will proudly (and profitably) wave Mickey's banner "high, high, high!"

Another example: D'Lites Restaurants closely resembled TGI Friday's, Bennigan's, Chili's, Applebee's and other casual dinner houses in the way their restaurants looked and how they were positioned. However, the major differences were that D'Lites didn't serve liquor...everything in their restaurants had to be "natural" (wall treatments, paper goods, condiments, etc.)...the restaurants were geared toward over-the-counter self-service...and also, D'Lites focused on a limited menu that was near-exclusively vegetarian. Close enough wasn't good enough. Their mid-scale price points weren't positioned to compete against self-serve fast food operators and they also had lots of trouble competing with full-service casual dine restaurants. When consumers went out to eat at a casual dine restaurant, they expected hospitality (service provided by waitresses and waiters), a broad choice of menu offerings (all kinds of foods and proteins) and they sought a variety of alcoholic beverages (beer, wine, mixed drinks, etc.). D'Lites didn't measure up. They came close in the way they looked but that just wasn't enough. D'Lites went bust!

The Major Indoor Soccer League (MISL) came close to living up to its name as a "major" professional sports league, however, "close" wins no cigars. Although they had franchises in New York and Los Angeles, most team cities were small, poor media markets such as Kansas City, Memphis, Nashville, St. Louis, Tacoma and Wichita. The MISL marketed mostly to children who played soccer as opposed to creating new adult fans with no soccer experience (After all, how many NFL or NBA or NHL fans actually played organized football, basketball or ice hockey?). I guess they forgot that the adult dollar was vitally important in building any sports franchise.

Member teams marketed the talents of many international soccer stars who not only couldn't speak English but who had names most Americans couldn't pronounce. Thus, American fans couldn't identify with the MISL athletes. Insignificant corporate sponsorship, inexpensive ticket prices (and lots of "freebies") and never anything more than a local market television deal made the League more "minor" than "major." There was also great imbalance in the League. The Kansas City Comets regularly sold out their 16,000 arena seats at Kemper Arena, while a more pivotal, major market franchise, the New York Arrows, averaged 3,500 attendees per game in the Nassau Coliseum. Indoor soccer is a fast-paced, high-action sport with lots of positive attributes. The Major Indoor Soccer League came real close, but close enough wasn't good enough. Despite their Herculean efforts, the League folded.

If I seem to be negative about getting "close" or putting forth a valiant "effort," it's because I am. In business, "close" means failure, "effort" means nothing and "results" mean everything. *Any company that rewards its people for "getting close" or putting forth good "effort" is in big trouble. Reward results or don't reward at all.*

No matter how "close" an athletic contest might be, in the end, the record book is black-and-white and simply shows either a big fat "W" for "Win" or a depressing little "L" for "Loss."

"Almost!" and "Good try!" and "Great effort!" and "Man, that was close..." are usually the battle cries of those whose team dropped the ball, missed an opportunity or lost a game.

There's no place in business for "close." You see, the world of business has its own "record book." More commonly called the "general ledger," instead of "W" or "L," accountants journal entry a big fat "P" for "Profit" (Win) or a depressing little "L" for "Loss."

Close enough is *not* good enough. Close enough is garbage!

Challenge the Myths of
Your Own Conventional Wisdom...

CHAPTER HIGHLIGHTS

- Close enough has never been good enough.
- Man has always endeavored for higher, faster, better and of course, closer.
- In our high-tech age of exactness, preciseness, correctness, and absolute "on the money-ness"...close enough is NOT good enough.

- In an age of technological preciseness, "Smart Bomb Marketing" is the only acceptable initiative. If it's not a "direct hit" today, it's NOT a hit!
- Everyone, every company makes mistakes.
- Any company that rewards its people for "getting close" or putting forth good "effort" is in big trouble. Reward results or don't reward at all.
- "Almost!" and "Good try!" and "Great effort!" and "Man, that was close..." are usually the battle cries of those whose team dropped the ball, missed an opportunity or lost a game.
- Close enough is NOT good enough. Close enough is...garbage!

◇

VALUE MEANS "CHEAP"

Here's the snapshot.

Burger King, Carl's Jr., Hardee's, McDonald's, Taco Bell and other quick-serve restaurants (QSRs) in the U.S. all made major investments in signage and advertising materials boldly announcing "VALUE MEALS" at their respective units.

Taco Bell's 39-cent taco "value meal deal" and Burger King's 49-cent hamburger "value meal" were designed to drive more customers into the restaurant (called "building traffic"), get more people to eat at these fast-food places (called "gaining trial from non-users") and create new customers (called "building frequency"). However, they also helped misguide America's children into thinking value means "cheap."

Value does not, in fact, mean cheap.

"Value" is often defined as "...meeting expectations" (getting what you paid for).

I, for one, believe energetic business-builders should expand this definition and look at value as "exceeding expectations." Writer Tom Peters called this kind of customer satisfaction *"wow."* Professor Ken Blanchard called it creating *"raving fans."*

Anyway you slice it, exceeding expectations is the headline.

Examples of "exceeding expectations" include:

- Providing your customer, consumer, patron or client a bag-full of new, exciting additional reasons to buy your products, programs or services...

- Providing your customer, consumer, patron or client ideas, information, actionable data and education...

- Providing your customer, consumer, patron or client marketing and selling solutions, not just products...

- Providing your customer, consumer, patron or client real partnering, sharing and assistance...

- Providing your customer, consumer, patron or client something extra, you know, the "*and more...*"

Too often, American businesses deceive themselves and believe they are adding value when in reality, they are adding costs and destroying value. For instance, allocating significant resources to collect data may be more on the "cost adding" side of the equation than the value creation side...especially "if" the data is not actionable.

———◇———

Adding costs often results in
value destruction, not value addition.
Value is also different things to different people.
It is situation specific and may even change
as an individual's needs, position
and situation changes.

———◇———

For example, I have a hairdresser named Veronica. She is excellent at what she does and the good news, for me, is that she knows this head of mine very well. That's valuable to me. She provides "added value" because Veronica also understands how dizzy and busy my life can be and squeezes my haircuts in between her other appointments...often getting me in and out of her beauty salon chair in twenty minutes.

Saving time is real value to me. I'm a fast-moving, dizzy, busy consultant, writer, speaker and educator. Save me time and you'll keep me as a customer.

Unfortunately, after going to Veronica's shop for a year, or so, I started noticing a familiarity building that started cutting (no pun intended) into the value she was delivering. You see, I found a direct inverse correlation to Veronica's hair cutting speed and her conversations. The more she talked, the slower she cut my hair.

I didn't go to her shop for chit-chat.

When speed is one critical success factor in my defining value, Veronica started destroying value through her endless chatter.

I certainly don't have anything against interaction and conversation. And Veronica is certainly a nice lady with a good personality. However, I didn't go to Veronica's shop for spirited conversation. I went there for fast, quality haircuts.

The haircuts started taking thirty minutes, then thirty-five minutes, soon forty minutes. I had no time to waste, yet, instead of providing me efficient clipping and snipping, Veronica was providing me the neighborhood news.

Unfortunately, just as many consumers have had to do, I was forced to help a vendor (in this case my hair stylist) reestablish value lost. Today, I sit in her chair, close my eyes and pretend to be sleeping while she cuts my hair. She's kind and considerate enough to cut without talking so as not to wake me up. High five! Hurrah! I have regained the value once lost, Veronica's kept me as a customer and we're both a value to each other.

The irony is that I had to help her help me receive the value I expected.

For your information, I am not sending Veronica an autographed copy of this book. I doubt if she would see any "value" in it anyway. Besides, if I did, I'm not sure I'd feel comfortable snoozing in her chair while she stood beside me with sharp scissors in her hand. I "value" my ears too much.

So....value doesn't mean "cheap." Value is also occasion, situation and consumer specific. And we constantly learn that those who create and provide value can slip (and in this case snip) and destroy value.

Case in point, we have all bemoaned the tragedy of our terribly impersonal, high-tech, low-touch telecommunications world that has us spending more time pushing telephone buttons than talking to a live human being for assistance. This is particularly true when calling an airline for information or reservations.

We've all heard messages such as "Kindly push button No. 1 if you're calling from a touch tone phone. Push button No. 2 if you're seeking information, No. 3 if you desire to make a reservation, No. 4 if you're seeking your frequent flyer balance, etc."

And it's not limited to airline messages. Hotels, department stores, telephone carriers, colleges, hospitals and other businesses seem to have all gone from "high touch" (human-to-human contact and conversation) to "high tech" (machine-based communication).

After a while, all this touch tone button pushing becomes very annoying, certainly not customer friendly and a source for both stress and consternation. In short, what started out to be an efficient way to provide value, customer service and to handle customer telephone calls...ended up as a frustrating example of high-tech value destruction.

Want to beat the button-pushing system? Simply hang on the line and make the robot believe you're dialing from a rotary phone. For whatever reason, the system seems to reward rotary phone users quickly by giving them a real live person to talk to.

In any event, this is value destruction at its finest.

"What good is a cow that gives milk and then kicks the can over?"

Let's go back to a fast food "value meal deal" example which turned out to be a major miss for McDonald's.

There is no restaurant chain in the world I respect more than McDonald's. Historically, they have been a consistent example of effective management, efficient systems, innovative programs, dynamic marketing, state-of-the-industry quality control, etc. However, even the best can drop the ball.

Their value meal deal, "Campaign 55," offered consumers a 55-cent sandwich with the purchase of french fries and a drink. It resulted in more value destruction than value creation.

First of all, when McDonald's initially introduced the campaign, it was difficult to understand. Consumers were confused. Could they buy any of McDonald's sandwiches or burgers for 55-cents? If not, which one was on "special," which wasn't? Secondly, there was additional confusion about whether the deeply discounted price was for just the sandwich or for a bundled "combo meal." Finally, as a result of the program, McDonald's customers started questioning the health of the chain. Could it be that the "golden arches" were feeling so much intense competitive pressure that they decided to give away meals at incredibly low prices to regain traffic?

This, coupled with their franchise community concerned about system-wide shrinking margins, national drops in same-store sales and "Campaign 55" failing to improve lunch and dinner capture rates all made for a tough few months for McDonald's.

What was originally intended to create value, actually confused customers, aggravated franchisees and ultimately destroyed value.

For producers, retailers and service merchants, providing real value is directly related to efficient, effective consumer targeting and bundling various alternative benefits packages to each group. Understanding target consumer demographics, psychographics, sociographics, per cap spending patterns and "need states" are critical in assessing value requirements and packaging the right value to deliver to the right consumer group.

Domino's Pizza rarely promotes flavor, assortment, quality nor price. Their value proposition was simple. "Thirty minutes or free!" Dizzy, busy, activity rich, time poor consumers on-the-run who need to quickly solve their dinner dilemmas receive value from Domino's speed of service.

In strategic planning sessions, Domino's looked at their potential pizza delivery consumer base in two segments: "consumers in a hurry" and "consumers *not* in a hurry." Domino's obviously targets the hassled "in a hurry" crowd. That's where they can provide the greatest value.

By the same token, just as a bigger assortment means bigger value to one consumer, a more focused shorter line of high quality offerings on display represent bigger value to another consumer.

F.A.O. Schwartz is positioned as the "everyanything" store for toys, merchandising a huge breadth and depth of offerings for the young (and young at heart). With a number of their locations in fast-paced, high-traffic urban environments, they decided they needed to develop a strategy for those consumers who might be "in a time crunch" by displaying a very convenient "best of" table in front of their stores (best of toys for boys, best of toys for girls) for quick and easy shopping.

Therefore, if a consumer had lots of time, F.A.O. Schwartz was certainly a wonderful place to browse. If, on the other hand, a consumer had only a little time to spare, these "in a crunch" consumers could walk right up to the F.A.O. Schwartz "best of" express table and view the fifteen or twenty products on display for an efficient, quicker shop. Both strategies worked because each provided a different kind of value for a different kind of consumer need state.

Lines from a song in the Gilbert and Sullivan operetta, "The Mikado," stated, "Let the punishment fit the crime."[21] For purposes of supporting this chapter's message, "Let the value fit the customer."

Save me time...save me money...make it convenient... provide me easy-to-use options...give me something unique...help me simplify my life (and business)...truly understand my business and help me grow...protect my margins...afford me access to new products and services...furnish me "hands on" information and linkage to new technology...deliver actionable data to me that will drive my business...provide me with a low-risk opportunity...establish a comfort zone for me...and exceed my expectations.

These each represent different types of value. Some are important to one kind of consumer. Others are not.

Let the customer and consumer pick their value package. "Let the value fit the customer."

I am always cynical when I hear companies put "price" and "value" in the same sentence...conveying that they're interchangeable terms. A good price is simply not "value!"

A wonderful Oscar Wilde definition of a "cynic" is "...a man who knows the price of everything and the value of nothing."

VALUE IS THE KEY

Value, then is the key...NOT pricing. However, moving from PRICE to VALUE may bring several additional consumer "cost drivers" into the equation. Obviously, there is a cost to "value-add." However, when a consumer measures the total cost of product consumption, including the added value, it must all lead to customer satisfaction as a package (not just a product and price).

Certainly price value relationships are important, however, if you live by the price you'll surely die by the price. A complex, mature marketplace sees many consumers seeking more than "just" a good product at a fair price. It's the "and more..." that builds long-term business, customer loyalty and volume.

———◇———

**Remember, value means meeting and,
it is hoped, exceeding, expectations.**

———◇———

Understanding that time is the currency of our lives and that dizzy, busy "time poor" consumers placed a high value on convenience, Coca-Cola is to be commended for developing its "Fast Lane Merchandiser," a convenient, refrigerated soft drink cooler placed right on the cashier check-out lines of supermarkets, drugstores and discount stores. A prime example of "intercept marketing," this merchandiser makes buying a refreshing cold beverage easy at an important in-store location ideal for impulse. Needless to say, "easy" is a value to consumers on the run.

Virgin Atlantic Airways is a terrific provider of value. Rather than go the route of other airlines and provide "extras" to just first class travelers, Virgin furnished value-added benefits to all classes of travel. For instance, extra space between rows...reclining seats...hot meals...even in-seat personal television units were standard benefits to coach, business and first class passengers alike. Why? Simply put, Virgin realized that if they provided "first class" value to all classes of travel, they would likely fill the entire plane. By selling all seats on its airplanes, Virgin benefited financially, both to the bottom line and by having a strong revenue stream capable of funding and adding more route schedule alternatives for travelers. In the end, offering travelers more flight alternatives was a huge value. That's what airplane customers seek, especially the business customer.

Thus, by creating value, as they have done, Virgin proved that the sum of the parts (coach, premium class and Upper Class™) can add up to a total greater than the whole (revenue and value).

In metropolitan New York, there is a fabulous chain of home furnishing stores called Fortunoff's. In a department store format, they offer high-end silverware, china, art, linens, decor items, pots, pans, placemats, centerpieces, crystal, window treatments and more. In fact, they even seem to specialize in the "and more..." Fortunoff's primary value to their very loyal customer base is the breadth and depth of their offerings. Whether you're decorating a house or seeking a unique wedding gift, Fortunoff's has it all. In fact, their "we have it all" value proposition states that if consumers are unable to find what they are seeking at Fortunoff's, the store will find the goods for the customer...even if it required Fortunoff's service representatives to go out and purchase items from a competitor.

For more than fifty years, the chain has had one primary marketing position: "Fortunoff's...the source!"

Over many successful years, Fortunoff's clearly communicated their value proposition to the community. Having it all and being the shopping source, Fortunoff's provides an abundance of value to its customers.

The value proposition, premise, program or package can't be vague. It must be clear and easily defined by consumers (i.e. Coca-Cola offers you value by providing convenient "fast lane" access to cold beverages; Virgin Atlantic Airways provides equal value to all passenger classes; Fortunoff's is a value to customers by being a single source; etc.).

Unfortunately, due to poor management and sub-par operational execution, we are oftentimes disappointed by many of our retailers, suppliers and vendors. As consumers, we accept disappointment too often and try hard to ignore substandard service. We all can identify with placing a drive-through window fast food order for a burger, fries and Coke only to realize, down the road a mile or two, we actually received a chicken filet sandwich, onion rings and a Sprite.

Value is obviously receiving what was promised. That seems simple enough, however, it's a stretch and a huge challenge for many businesses. We have no shortage nor deficiency of ideas, information, knowledge and data. Our primary gap and deficiency is on the execution side of the equation.

Individuals who...and companies that obsess with efficiently delivering on their commitments and consistently, effectively execute will win, long term.

No, value doesn't mean cheap. Far from it.

Value is, perhaps, the single most important reason why customers trust a brand, frequent an establishment and continually buy a product.

Challenge the Myths of
Your Own Conventional Wisdom...

CHAPTER HIGHLIGHTS

- "Value" does not, in fact, mean cheap.

- "Value" is often defined as "...meeting expectations" (getting what you paid for). Energetic business-builders should expand this definition and look at value as "exceeding expectations."

- Often, American businesses deceive themselves and believe they are adding value when in reality, they are adding costs and destroying value.

- Adding costs often result in value destruction, not value addition.

- Value is also different things to different people. It's occasion related and may even change as an individual's needs, position and situation changes.

- What good is a cow that gives milk and then kicks the can over?

- Let the customer and consumer pick their value package. Value is a very personal thing.

- Value is, perhaps, the single most important reason why customers trust a brand, frequent an establishment and continually buy a product.

◇

THE BEST OFFENSE IS A GOOD DEFENSE

"The best offense is a good defense!" That's absurd. That's preposterous. That's ridiculous.

Imagine legendary football coaches Bear Bryant (Alabama), Knute Rockne (Notre Dame) and Vince Lombardi (Green Bay Packers) reacting to that philosophy (myth).

The Bear once said, "The only, only way to win is by owning the football!"

Rockne told a reporter at the Chicago Tribune, "Good defenses are designed for two purposes...to stop the enemy and to get the ball back. And we must have the ball back to win. Period!"

And "Papa" Vince boldly announced, "To win, you must have a continuous obsession with continuous possession!"

Offense is the key. Get the ball...rip and tear and scratch and scrape and fight for control (of the ball, of the business, etc.). "Having," "owning," "possessing" and "controlling" are words that represent the most viable ways to succeed and score.

There's an awful lot to be said about declaring victory, about being PROactive (as in PROfessional) and constantly moving on the offense in business building.

Note, however, this requires a highly focused, positive mental attitude. The roots of a strong offense are optimism, boldness, positivism, goal orientation and an overriding need to score points and win.

An offensive nature and culture also require business people to redefine their concept of "risk."

———◇———

The old, provincial way of viewing risk is
best illustrated by the question,
What is the risk we're taking if we DO that?

———◇———

The new, take-the-ball-on-offense-and-run-with-it attitude is defined by a more relevant, risk-oriented question, *What is the risk we're taking if we DON'T DO that?*

———◇———

Coca-Cola went on the offense very early in the "cola wars" and declared victory. Globally announcing through the media that "Coke is it!" and "Coke is the real thing!," it positioned every competing soft drink as an imitation, as an upstart, as No 2.

"Coke" has become virtually generic for "cola."

I've never heard anyone ask a bartender for a "rum and cola," or a "rum and Pepsi." It's always been a "rum and Coke." It will likely always be a rum and Coke. I must admit, however, Pat Burgess, my mother-in-law, often orders a toddy by asking her country club bartender for, and I quote, "a rum and Coke with Pepsi, please."

Hertz did the same thing in the auto rental game. Although Avis launched a spirited "We're No. 2. We try harder!" campaign, Hertz has played "ball control" aggressively on offense for over three decades with great success.

In a young distribution channel or when marketing a relatively new product category or capitalizing on an emerging trend...going on offense is simply declaring victory and assuming the position of "leader." In reality, it's grabbing the position of leader...and aggressively going on offense.

Don't ask. Grab the ball and hold on tightly. There's no place for etiquette here. Grab the business and drive harder and harder for greater results.

Where there are no rules (i.e., product configuration, package form, price point, etc.), create rules. Leaders define, refine, invent, invigorate and interestingly enough, LEAD!

It sounds almost sophomoric but in order for a company to be competitive, it must be able to compete. And the will as well as lust for competition comes from an offensive psyche.

Offense is also about shooting for scores to put "points on the board" (objectives, targets, goals, etc.).

Pro hockey's "Great One," Wayne Gretzky, once said, "I miss 100 percent of the shots I never take."

I'm often reminded of my days coaching my seven-year-old son Eric's YMCA basketball team. For your information (or recollection), seven–year-old youth basketball is characterized by kids shooting the ball high into the air only to have the ball return back and hit them in the face. Big scores are 10 to 8, etc.

Well, we had a perfect record that year. Yes, under my leadership (they called me "Coach B"), Eric's team was 0-7. By the way, if you're not a big sports fan, 0-7 is not really a very terrific season.

Coming back from our seventh loss, I noticed Eric was upset. I turned to my boy and said, "Eric...don't be sad. It's only a game, son. It's only a game..." is an obligatory expression used by losing coaches, just like, "It's only a customer..." is an obligatory expression used by losing (and loser) business managers.

In fact, I am convinced that the person who originally said, "It's only a game" lost.

Back to my story. Eric responded, "Dad, I'm not upset about the game. I'm upset that in seven games I haven't scored a basket. I just want to know what it feels like."

Hitting me like a splash of ice water, I realized I let Eric (and the entire team) down. In my coaching, mentoring and teaching, I never told the kids the most important rule in basketball...actually, the most important rule in business...in fact, the most important rule in life. *You cannot score unless you shoot!*

I turned to Eric and said, "Eric...in seven games, son, you haven't taken a shot. You cannot score unless you shoot."

Well, a light bulb went on in my son's head. He got it. He truly got it.

I had to miss game number eight due to an out-of-town trip and called in late in the afternoon that next Saturday. Eric answered the phone and I asked, "Eric, how'd we do today...how did the game go?"

Excitedly he exclaimed, "Dad, Dad...we won our first game, 10 to 8, and I scored all 10 points!"

Now I was thrilled for the team and incredibly thrilled (and proud) of my son. I started thinking "Move over Michael Jordan...here comes Eric Blumenthal!" Visions of kids singing "I want to be like Eric..." and Eric's name on shorts and shirts and sneakers and Eric becoming the next highly paid, highly endorsed megastar, and...hey, wait a minute!

It dawned on me that the team lost seven games in a row while I coached them.

I left town and wham...they won!

I asked Eric, "Tell me, what did Coach Paul do to fire up the team?" Coach Paul, as you might guess, was my assistant coach, my friend, my cul de sac buddy, my neighbor...

Eric sheepishly responded, "Dad....Coach Paul got the flu. Mom coached the team!"

Wham...bam...thank you coach ma'am!

Mom coached the team!

Needless to say, it was an incredible experience for me when I returned to coach the team the following week and to hear all the women in the bleachers chant, "We want Kim! We want Kim!"

Nonetheless, the lesson is an important one. In fact, the lesson is critically important. You cannot score unless you shoot.

In most cases, you cannot score unless you're on offense.

It's simple. It's vital!

It's also important to note that offense manages the tempo of the game. Offense manages the action. Defenses typically react and respond. When confronted with the choice of managing or being managed, I like managing. Offense is in charge!

The question logically arises, "What are the keys to successful offense?"

To successfully launch and build an offensive campaign and culture, every good coach and manager needs a few alternative "game plans" and base strategies. I believe an offensive plan portfolio should hold three distinct plan models. They are oriented toward

- Core Competencies
- Situation-Specifics
- Competitive Opportunities

The first model is based on team (company) "core competencies." Certainly logical and appropriate, this offensive plan should be constructed around the assets, equities, special abilities, capacity, skill sets and capabilities of the team (organization). This core or base business plan guides the offensive initiative through well-defined guiding principles, highly organized strategies and a rock solid set of standards, practices, policies and procedures.

Outsiders (including competitors) should be able to readily verbalize and define this plan as a specific type of offense and a special style of business development. Citing a few examples, here are some phrases observers have used to define three very different companies and their particular, individual offensive sets, all based on core competencies...

- "They are known for a run and gun offense. They move very fast, very fast! Moving targets are tough to hit. They crank out an idea and product and program every minute. They're lightning fast." (said about Microsoft by one of their many competitors)
- "They're killers! They have a take-no-prisoners attitude and positioning. It's all or nothing. They are not content with just a piece of the business. They must have it all. Period!" (said about Wal-Mart Super Centers by a competing supermarket chain operator)
- "They're everywhere! Focusing on every conceivable distribution channel, they're clearly a ubiquity-oriented company. It's tough to keep up with all they do and with all their points of distribution." (said about Hallmark Cards by one of their key competitors)

Where the first offensive plan option is based on the "core competencies" of the team, the second offensive positioning is one based on a specific game, or market "situation."

An important skill set and trait of a successful leader is the ability of the leader (coach, director, manager, et. al.) to be agile and flexible. Constantly doing a "situation analysis" and responding with a quick repositioning plan is vital. It's obvious that things change quickly and when they do change, the "same old, same old" plan and offensive strategy may lose its meaning and relevancy.

Slightly altering or even dramatically altering an offensive scheme and blueprint is solely dependent upon the situation at hand.

In some situations, there might be a need for management to move people to different territories to meet distinct customer needs, or to provide added value, or to consider matching competitive initiatives (this is where offense and defense blur a bit). Situations may require launching a product earlier than previously planned or perhaps holding back a product launch for situation-specific reasons.

THE "RE" WORDS

Here's where my favorite prefix, "re," comes into play again.

The following represent a handful of "re" words that relate well to situation-oriented offense:

- reallocating (as in resources),
- rearranging (as in priorities),
- redefining (as in positioning),
- redeploying (as in people placement),
- redesigning (as in programs),
- re-engineering (as in product offering),
- re-entering (as in marketplaces),
- reintroducing (as in process),
- regrouping (as in modifying a plan),
- reorganizing (as in managing), and
- re, re, re and more re...

Situation-driven offense is all about adapting, adjusting, altering and reshaping plans prior to a specific situation...during a particular situation...or directly and immediately after a situation has occurred.

The third strategic option for offense is based on "competitive opportunities."

I don't believe an enterprise should obsess with the competition, but I do believe it is appropriate, prudent and wise to understand the competition...especially in terms of their management style, organizational structure, production capabilities, market positioning, product lines, resources and more. The "and more" is also understanding the enemy in terms of a traditional template referred to as "SWOPT," namely, strengths, weaknesses, opportunities, problems and threats.

Using the "competitive opportunities" approach to offense simply means playing your strengths against the competitor's weaknesses. It's an opportunistic oriented offense. Run to daylight. Find an opening and fill it.

If the competition is financially strapped and you have "deep pockets," that might warrant an offensive initiative based on discounting, heavy promoting, sampling, etc. On the other hand, if the competition has a coverage gap in a particular market due to employee turnover, that might lead to a different kind of offensive initiative such as a major market media campaign, or an in-market sales blitz or even the deployment of additional personnel.

WHAT DOES A COMPANY WITH A WELL-DEFINED OFFENSIVE POSITION LOOK LIKE?

Some real examples of companies with well-defined offensive positions, you ask? Here are two for review.

THE "BOLD, BRASH JUST-TRY-TO-BEAT-ME" OFFENSIVE POSITION

The Men's Warehouse, a chain of clothing stores, is famous for constantly making bold, brash marketing claims that have kept them on both the offense and "cutting edge." For instance, if a customer prospect finds a comparable brand name suit sold by any other store for a lower price than The Men's Warehouse, they will match and beat the price. Their advertisements constantly throw the gauntlet down against all competitors challenging each...almost begging each of them...for some competition. One of their offensive strategic planks is the bold assertion and position that the competition absolutely cannot measure up against them. They dare the competition to try. In all of their advertisements, they confidently promise consumers that they will always measure up, win and exceed expectations. In fact, at the close of every communication piece (electronic or print), their president, George Zimmer, assures consumers The Men's Warehouse will deliver on their promises and he closes each commercial with, "I'm the company president and I guarantee it!"

THE "I'M GOING TO DISTRIBUTE MY GOODS EVERYWHERE" OFFENSE

Robert Woodruff, the longtime president of Coca-Cola (served in that capacity from 1923 to 1965), is credited for creating, developing and espousing the primary Coke offensive position referred to, appropriately, as "W.A.R." An acronym for "Within Arm's Reach," Coke's aspiration is to be "within arm's reach" of desire. In other words, if one is thirsty and desires a cold, refreshing soft drink, regardless of where one might be, a Coca-Cola product should be readily accessible...you know, within arm's reach. This is a ubiquitous strategy. It boldly says, "I'm going to distribute my beverage products everywhere." Case in point, Coke products globally can be found in convenience stores, mass merchandisers, arenas, stadiums, restaurants, warehouse clubs, public use areas, college campuses, supermarkets, airports, bus terminals, vending machines, in-flight on airplanes, in malls...any and every possible place where there are people.

———◇———

Companies with well-defined offensive positions are usually successful.

———◇———

Domino's Pizza boldly declared victory as the most efficient pizza delivery network in the U.S. "Thirty minutes delivered piping hot to your front door or we'll give you your money back," they announced. They were efficient and their game plan proved effective.

Southwest Airlines went on the offense and proclaimed that less is actually more. Eliminating food service, as well as other "frills," their aggressive selling proposition was based on great service, the lowest fares imaginable and a dedication to "on time" arrivals. "Fly Southwest Airlines for peanuts!" they said and as well as offering incredibly low fares, consistent with their theme, they also served only peanuts to their passengers in-flight. They have been hugely successful.

American Express, Citicorp, Disney, Hallmark Cards, Hewlett Packard, IBM, Intel, Johnson & Johnson, Merck, Microsoft, Mirage Resorts, Motorola, Sony, Wal-Mart and UPS are fifteen additional examples of companies that are category leaders, are consistent winners and constantly remain on offense. Read about them. Study them. There's lots that can be learned.

Offense comes in different shapes, forms, styles and initiatives.

As opposed to the traditional practice of what I call "defensive hiring," you know, advertising for employee candidates by way of providing a boring job description "write up" in a publication, seemingly requiring the candidate need only have a pulse to apply...I read a blind advertisement in a national newspaper by a company seeking to provide a career opportunity for, and I quote, "...a lively, energetic, positive, quick-witted, highly motivated, passionate marketing person who can demonstrate generating an idea-a-minute and who can prove a successful history of innovation, creativity and making a difference in the consumer goods business."

Wow! That's offense.

Sounding like the kind of newspaper employment section ads I've read over the years put forth by the likes of Crate & Barrel, Disney, Nike, Delta Airlines and Nordstrom, the company that placed this ad is obviously spirited and offensively-minded.

I like that. The world likes that. They're probably a real winner!

———◇———

Winners understand the critical importance of offense.

———◇———

If you accept the premise that business is war, you're also likely to realize that *in war, there are no prizes nor medals for second place.*

The best offense is not a good defense. The best offense is a great offense.

Challenge the Myths of Your Own Conventional Wisdom...

CHAPTER HIGHLIGHTS

- The best offense is a good defense. That's absurd, preposterous and ridiculous.

- The old, provincial way of viewing risk is best defined by the question, *What is the risk we're taking if we DO that?* The new, take-the-ball-on-offense-and-run-with-it attitude is defined by a more relevant, risk-oriented question, *What is the risk we're taking if we DON'T DO that?*

- Don't ask. Grab the ball and hold on tightly.

- Where there are no rules, create rules.

- I am convinced that the person who originally said, "It's only a game" lost.

- You cannot score unless you shoot!

- There are three distinct offensive plan models for business-builders, namely:
  ◇ Core Competencies
  ◇ Situation-Specifics
  ◇ Competitive Opportunities

- An important skill set and trait of a successful leader is the ability of the leader (coach, director, manager, et. al.) to be agile and flexible.

- Focus aggressively on the prefix "re" (i.e., reallocating, rearranging, redefining, redeploying, reorganizing, etc.).

- Better understanding BOTH your assets and deficits as well as the assets and deficits of the competition can be accomplished by developing a comprehensive "SWOPT" analysis.
  S   Strengths
  W   Weaknesses
  O   Opportunities
  P   Problems
  T   Threats

- Companies with well-defined offensive positions are usually successful.

- Winners understand the critical importance of offense.

- In war, there are no prizes nor medals for second place.

- The best offense is not a good defense. The best offense is a great offense.

◇

WATCH THE COMPETITION CLOSELY

Don't look back!

In "Chariots of Fire," the wonderful movie about running and runners, there was a particularly memorable scene when the key character was leading an important sprint race, only to lose at the finish line. In reviewing stop-action photos of the race with his coach, it became crystal clear to the runner that he relinquished his lead when he turned his head and looked back to see how the competition was doing.

He "looked back."

Don't ever, ever look back!

———◇———

Run your own race. Play your own game. Focus exclusively on your own business activities and performance.

———◇———

Looking back, as in the movie scene described above, makes you lose concentration, "break stride" and fragment your focus.

Once you've created your own "game plan" (or "business plan" or "life plan"), commit to your strategies and tactics and aggressively, energetically, passionately pursue excellence through effective, efficient execution.

I believe gathering competitive intelligence is important. I believe watching the "game films" are also important. However, in the end, developing your very own strategy with solid rationale, commitment and passion...and obsessively working to implement that strategy...is the way to win.

Be smart (and agile) enough to alter plans when necessary. Be savvy enough to adapt and adjust to market conditions when appropriate. Be committed enough to plan your work and work your plan.

Successful business ventures (and adventures) start with an overriding corporate confidence that "we can" and "we will." Believing in your company, products, programs and good people (including yourself) must be fundamental.

If there is no belief, there will be no business building. Period!

"Declare victory" very early in the process...even before the first initiative missile is launched.

Obviously, this leads to a reliance, faith and trust that your plans and business development activities are in order, are on target and poised for success.

———◇———

Your success has nothing to do with the "other guy."

———◇———

Achievement is totally dependent upon your execution, implementation and performance. Focus on continuous improvement, beating yourself and besting your previous performances, not on beating the competition. If you continue to improve, raise the bar, excel and surpass your own performances, you'll be the best you can possibly be and ultimately...you'll succeed.

———◇———

I ascribe to what I've called "The 5-95 Rule."
In short, everything in life (and business) is 5 percent idea and
95 percent work (and effective execution).

———◇———

You don't own an exclusive on ideas. It's likely that everyone of your competitors will have similar "ideas" and "brainstorms." However, it's the execution that separates good ideas from good business initiatives.

Forget the competition. Focus on your own efficient, effective execution.

For instance, in 1993, on a business trip to the West Coast, I was staying at the Hyatt Hotel in Irvine, California.

I woke up about 6 a.m. so I could read the newspaper, then go for a morning jog. I pulled out what I thought was *USA Today* from under my hotel room door. (Ever try getting the newspaper from under your hotel room door in your underwear, with the fear that the door might close behind you, leaving you on the hall side of the door in your boxers? That's got to be the fear of every business traveler, no?) Instead of *USA Today*, under my door was *The Japanese Times*.

I looked up and down the hallway and sure enough, everyone on my floor had the *USA Today* in front of their doors except for me.

Something was wrong. Certainly "Blumenthal" was not a Japanese name. I couldn't figure it out.

I called down to the hotel manager's office to find out why I had received the Japanese paper. He was embarrassed and said, "I'm terribly sorry, Mr. Blumenthal. You see we have seventy-five guests from Tokyo staying at the hotel. They read and speak no English and we thought, in the name of hospitality, we'd provide them with a newspaper they might enjoy."

I thought that was an incredible idea. Think about it..."in the name of hospitality"...What a wonderful, creative, brilliant idea.

Although the idea was terrific, the execution was lousy—absolutely terrible! After all, as it turned out, the Japanese visitors all received *USA Today* and all the American guests received *The Japanese Times*.

It all gets down to a very simple fact of business life. Success comes from the *execution* of sound ideas.

How you set your strategic, tactical and attack plans for execution will ultimately define your destination and endgame.

There is no deficit of ideas, information and knowledge in our world today. As illustrated by the Japanese newspaper story, however, there seems to be a huge deficit in our ability to effectively and efficiently execute.

And execution is purely dependent on *you*, not the other guy, the other team, another company...not the competition.

If we slammed resources against more effective execution and flawless implementation instead of costly competitive analysis, we'd likely be more successful (and more fulfilled).

When you focus on the competition, your mind plays tricks on you. You create unwarranted fear, conjure up distorted images and move off focus.

For instance, when I was playing high school football in Oceanside, New York, I remember a particular Saturday morning when my Dad drove me to the school before a game against a feared rival. As we approached the school, we passed the football stadium and in the distance I saw what I thought was the visiting team practicing on an adjacent field.

I wasn't wearing my glasses and squinted in disbelief. They looked huge. They looked incredibly huge. They were monsters!

I turned to my father and said something like, "Dad, those guys are going to maul us. Look at the size of that team!"

He smiled, drove into the parking lot and moved our car close enough for me to realize that the "team" I thought I saw on the field practicing wasn't the visiting team at all. It was only our high school band rehearsing their routine before the game.

When you focus on the competition, your mind (in this case, eyes) plays tricks on you.

I once read a quote by consultant Michael McKinley that read, "You will never have to worry about the competition if they think you're the competition!"

Forget "them." Strive for excellence and you'll ultimately succeed—in spite of the competition.

Focus on your own unique game and program. Creatively visualize your product, project, program or activity succeeding gloriously. Dream of the victory. Imagine the excitement, feel the fervor and pretend to visualize reaping the rewards of your efforts.

If you can dream it, you can do it, but you can't do it if you waste valuable energy and time concentrating on the "other guy."

THERE IS NO COMPETITION

In reality, there is no "competition." Every contest should be a contest between you and you. Work to increase *your* market share; commit to improving upon *your* own efficiency; *strive to outsell yourself...build on your previous successes and diligently work to best yourself.*

Break your own records.

Business (and career) building is *not* about besting the competition. Focus aggressively on continuous self improvement. Beat yourself.

Positive mental attitude, referred to as "PMA" in the late 1970s, is the key. Believe you can and you will. It matters not what others are doing.

A football coach back in 1963 stuck in my helmet a poem as a pre-game motivator. I still have that tattered and torn anonymous poem, titled: "It's All In A State Of Mind."

> If you think you are beaten you are.
> If you think you dare not you won't.
> If you like to win but don't think you can,
> It's almost a cinch you won't.
> Life's battles don't always go
> To the bigger or stronger man,
> But sooner or later the man who wins
> Is the fellow who thinks he can.
>
> Think big and your deeds will grow.
> Think small and you'll fall behind.
> Think that you can and you will.
> It's all in a state of mind.

So, look ahead—positively, energetically and with enthusiasm.

Clearly, it is all in a state of mind.

Satchel Paige, a star of the early Negro Baseball leagues and a legendary Hall of Fame pitcher, said it best, "Don't look back. Something will be gaining on you. Don't ever look back!"

Certainly I believe there's a place for "market intelligence" and "research," however, I believe the more you actually learn about competitive sets and activities...the more you learn about what direction you should or should not take yourself. Competitive intelligence serves well as a background for business building and brings a sense of context to your own work.

So many businesses spend lots of money on competitive research and analysis that studies everything the "other guy" is doing or is likely to do. I often wonder how much greater business growth might be if companies slammed those very same resources against action in the form of going/growing forward initiatives and virtually ignored the competition.

———◇———

If all you do is look back, you will surely drop back.

———◇———

People have a unique knack for talking themselves into things, especially as it relates to the power of foes.

I remember hearing an interesting story about a guy who needed a special wrench to fix his lawn mower. He turned to his wife and said, "Honey, I'm gonna go next door and borrow that hex box wrench from George."

He walked a few paces, stopped in his tracks and then said to her, "You know, I'm not sure about this. George always makes me feel so damn guilty when I borrow something. Maybe I shouldn't go to him. Ah...what the heck, I'll go see him."

Again, starting for the door, he abruptly stopped, turned to his wife and said, "I can't do it. I can't do it. Darn George makes me feel like a heel every time I ask him for anything. I won't be subjected to his crap. I cannot, nor will not...but honey, I really need that wrench. I'll just grit my teeth and let him make his remarks...yes, I've decided regardless of his attitude, I'm going for the wrench."

He slowly walked out of their house, then quickly returned and exclaimed to his wife, "That's it! That's it! I can't do it, babe. I just cannot move myself to go to that jerk and...and...oh, that idiot drives me crazy. Oh well, I'll give it a try even though I know what's gonna happen. Good-bye!"

Mumbling to himself all the way to George's house, anticipating negativism from George, he grew angrier and angrier. The nerve of George, he thought, to belittle him and make him feel guilty for borrowing the wrench.

Finally, he rang George's doorbell a number of times, pushing the button very aggressively.

When George came to the door, he angrily looked him in the eyes, blurted out "I don't want your damn wrench anyway!" and punched the highly surprised George in the nose.

We talk ourselves into things, including defeat, especially as it relates to formidable competitors.

————◇————

We can be our own worst enemy!

————◇————

The cartoon strip character Pogo once said, "We've met the enemy and they are us!"

Play your own game. Stick to your own plan. Commit to your own core ideology and spend time, effort and resources continually improving "you"...not constantly watching "them."

One of the great fallacies of watching the competition is the distinct possibility that the competition could be making major mistakes you're likely to imitate. Who is to say that the competition is doing anything right?

In an episode of television's classic show, "Leave It To Beaver," Theodore Cleaver (the "Beaver") was attending a school sponsored sit-down dinner. He wasn't sure about the rules of etiquette and asked his mother for advice. Mrs. Cleaver ("June" to those of you who were fans) simply said, "Honey, just watch what the other kids do and copy them. Just follow their lead. You'll do fine." Well, as luck would have it, Beaver's eyes were glued to a child he was convinced had proper table manners. When the child accidentally spilled soup all over his pants and started screaming about being scalded, Beaver assumed this was the right thing to do and purposely spilled his own bowl of soup, screaming as well.

Dumb example? Of course, but what would you expect from television. Still, the example makes an important point. Don't imitate, innovate!

Speaking of television, I often think about a conversation portrayed in Woody Allen's movie, "Annie Hall."[22] In the movie, Allen's friend, a California resident, was boasting about the merits of living in Southern California and said to the character being played by Woody, something to the effect of, "Isn't it beautiful here? Look at the streets. There's absolutely no garbage on the streets of Hollywood." Paraphrasing Allen's response, he said, "You're right—there's no garbage on Hollywood streets. That's 'cause they take the garbage and make it into television shows!"

Look, we all know there are certainly exceptions to every rule and every myth. Just as there are good, as well as bad, TV shows...there are good, as well as bad, times to focus on the competition.

Never surveying, studying, observing, even imitating the competition would be foolhardy. There's a time for everything. However, watching the competition should never become an obsession. It should also never become the primary motivation for specific plans, programs, products and strategies.

In fact, history shows that totally ignoring the competition can be disastrous. Case in point, Xerox ignored the glut of competitors coming into its markets from Asia and didn't take the competitive threats seriously. As a result, Xerox lost nearly $3 billion dollars in market value in the mid-1990s. By the same token, Sears never even considered Wal-Mart and Kmart competitors and conversely, didn't watch them, didn't study them and likely didn't acknowledge them until about 1992, the year Sears lost nearly $4 billion and saw both Kmart and Wal-Mart sales numbers blow far past their own volume. That year, Sears grossed $32 billion, Kmart grossed $39 billion and Wal-Mart grossed $55 billion. This was surely a case where watching the competition would have been smart.

Then, of course, there's the General Motors story. They took their eyes off both the wheel and the road by not watching the intricate, ingenious strategies being put forth by Japanese auto makers. GM refused to believe Americans would ever buy small cars and were convinced that anything "Made In Japan" couldn't measure up to GM's superior production standards. A $23.5 billion dollar loss in 1992 wasn't totally attributed to the competition, but certainly "some" of GM's huge shortfall went in the coffers of competitors GM refused to watch, much less acknowledge.

Still, more often than not...following the leader, emulating the competition, and doing what the other guy does can be a big mistake, especially if the model you're imitating is making its own mistakes.

Insecurity and lack of confidence are two major reasons why business people spend more time and energy obsessing about the competition than energetically innovating in their own businesses. It's vital to believe in yourself, your company, your products and your programs everyday...every single day.

Believing in a corporate, as well as career, mission, coupled with accepting total responsibility for efforts and actions put forth are two major steps toward building confidence.

Tom Sullivan, a friend and mentor, has a neat philosophy he refers to as "P.R.I.D.E." In short, in order to succeed, each one of us must have it to succeed. Sullivan's P.R.I.D.E. stands for

P   Personal

R   Responsibility for

I   Individual

D   Daily

E   Effort

Once people accept personal responsibility for their own individual daily efforts, they're on the road to becoming dependent upon themselves to succeed...and not concerned about any company, person or outside influence.

None of us can control the actions of others. We can only control our own action, effort and focus. If we accept this, then we'll also accept the premise that the importance of "watching the competition" is a major myth. I, for one, believe that the only competition we'll ever truly have is ourselves and the only record we need to think about breaking is our own last performance.

Don't look back!

Challenge the Myths of Your Own Conventional Wisdom...

CHAPTER HIGHLIGHTS

- Don't look back!
- Run your own race. Play your own game. Focus exclusively on your own business activities and performance.
- Be smart (and agile) enough to alter plans when necessary. Be savvy enough to adapt and adjust to market conditions when appropriate. Be committed enough to plan your work and work your plan.
- If there is no belief, there will be no business building. Period!
- Your success has nothing to do with the "other guy."

- "The 5-95 Rule" states that everything in life (and business) is 5 percent idea and 95 percent work (and effective execution).

- You don't own an exclusive on ideas. It's likely that everyone of your competitors will have similar "ideas" and "brainstorms." However, it's the execution that separates good ideas from good business initiatives.

- Forget the competition. Focus on your own efficient, effective execution.

- There is no deficit of ideas, information and knowledge in our world today. However, there is a huge deficit of effective implementation worldwide. Ideas alone are nothing. Couple them with kick 'em in the pants implementation and you're on the your way!

- When you focus on the competition, your mind plays tricks on you. You build unwarranted fear, conjure up distorted images and move off focus.

- In reality, there is no "competition." Every contest should be a contest between you and you. Work to increase *your* market share...commit to improving upon *your* own efficiency...strive to outsell *yourself*...build on *your* previous successes and diligently work to best *yourself.*

- Believe you can and you will.

- Look ahead...positively, energetically and with enthusiasm. Success is, clearly, all in a state of mind.

- If all you do is look back, you will surely drop back.

- We can be our own worst enemy!

- Don't look back!

◇

MYTH THIRTEEN

PLAY IT SAFE

**"Hey Wilbur! Hey Orville!
Are you guys nuts? If God wanted man to fly,
he'd have put wings on his body instead of arms."**

Someone had to have said that to the Wright brothers in Kitty Hawk, North Carolina. After all, it's human nature to come up with all the reasons why something can't be done, as opposed to coming up with all the reasons something can be done.

Can you imagine life without air travel? I, for one, would be out of business.

Consider this: Take away our air travel and you take away our frequent flyer points. Take away our frequent flyer points and we'd have to save real money to pay for our vacation trips.

No thanks!

———◇———

History books are filled with important stories of great achievements performed by visionaries who defied the rules and ignored the "play it safe" myth.

———◇———

No, I'm not a proponent of breaking municipal rules and laws. On the other hand, I am, in fact, a staunch advocate of rethinking and re-evaluating natural laws and the constraining, restraining rules of man in enterprise. Evolution? Revolution? It all depends.

I'm am a proponent of growth and progress.

When I was a child, I enjoyed playing the children's game, "Mother, May I?" You remember? "Mother, may I take two giant steps? May I do a bunny hop? Mother, may I take three baby steps or do two banana splits?, etc."

Many of us were raised to ask permission to "be excused" from the dinner table, as well as trained to raise our hand requesting permission from our teachers to "go to the lavatory" (restroom). With all this permission-oriented training, it's no small wonder that so many business people avoid making decisions, can't make decisions or desperately need "permission" to act. And when they do finally act, they probably "play it safe!"

I'd hate to think of how much moss would have grown and how much rust would have developed on products, projects and programs over the years because a visionary, an inventor or an innovator had to wait for permission to create, develop, test or produce.

Consider this...Henry Ford's bankers told him, "...it doesn't seem like the right time to develop your horse-less carriage." Pizza Hut's executive committee vehemently disagreed with founder Frank Carney's vision to deliver pizza and close down their "red roofs." Chrysler's Board of Directors initially frowned on the idea of replacing station wagons with new age "mini-vans."

Media power players all scoffed at Ted Turner's vision for cable television's importance...then laughed at his very notion that an all-news network (i.e., CNN) could succeed. Most money sources would not "permit" loans to fund his cable "pipe dreams."

Permission is a lever. When it comes to levers, I say "pull...or be pulled!" If in doubt, do!

In 1954, Sony boldly announced to the world that its primary objective was to change the world's viewpoint on products produced in Japan from "cheap," "junk," "poor quality," "unimportant," "toys," and "low tech"...to..."valued," "important," "high-tech," "state-of-the-art," "high quality," etc. This was an incredibly bold position for Sony to take, yet, they granted themselves permission to demonstrate to the entire world Japan's new orientation toward quality.

Why should any enterprise "play it safe" and waste time (and emotion) asking for permission?

Go for it. Grow from it! It's all about a passion for reinvention and redefinition.

As indicated earlier in this book, I firmly believe that the most important prefix in the English language is "re."

- Re-adjust
- Re-administer
- Re-advise
- Re-arrange
- Re-cycle
- Re-define
- Re-engineer
- Re-evaluate
- Re-inforce
- Re-invigorate
- Re-juvenate
- Re-market
- Re-position
- Re-work

...etc.

Re-, re- and more re-...that's the way to go, and grow. NY Yankee baseball great, Yogi Berra, said, "If it ain't broke, don't fix it." Well, the truth of the matter is, "If it ain't broke," it's probably tired, worn and in need of REpair and REthinking. Quite frankly, I am a proponent of the philosophy that says, "If it ain't broke, break it."

Man created and authored "the rules." It's appropriate, therefore, for man to have the option to obliterate those very same rules...especially those that are no longer realistic nor relevant.

For instance, the "man's not supposed to fly" natural rule limited and inhibited us from soaring like eagles and developing a mode of travel a lot more efficient than cars, trains or boats. It obviously would have been safer to walk, hop aboard a train or drive a car to our destination. However, following the rules and playing it safe contradicts the concepts of progress and innovation.

Tradition Reconsidered

The fact is traditional ways of doing things may become outdated. Faxes, Federal Expresses, Internet, online communication, voicemail and electronic commerce all broke some tried and true, traditional process and rule—for the betterment of us all.

When asked in an interview what his favorite business-building activity was, Nike founder and chairman Phil Knight replied, "I like to break things!"

Nike broke the rules. Along with the leadership of its co-founder, Bill Bowerman, the legendary track coach at the University of Oregon and Nike's first major "endorsement," Steve Prefontaine, the great U.S. Olympic long-distance runner, Nike helped create the running (and jogging) craze that became an enduring component of fitness programs for average people of all ages. Pre-Nike, consumers didn't run or jog for fitness. They exercised and they played sports. Running was something done only as a sport or when being chased by a dog.

They also swiftly moved from a sneaker company to a lifestyle company. Their extended product line includes all kinds of garments and accessories (i.e. sunglasses, watches, etc.). They even established retail stores that compete with the very retailers that market, merchandise and sell Nike products (enter "Nike Town").

Their brand is nearly ubiquitous and has become a lifestyle brand.

For instance, my son Jeffrey has a retainer in his mouth (a device one uses after long months of wearing braces) with a "Carolina Blue" Nike check ("Swoosh") on it. Yes...I'm serious! Nike is everywhere...even in Jeffrey's mouth!

Consumers are buying Nike shirts, pants, jackets, balls, hats, sunglasses, as well as shoes. Nike rewrote the rule book even though there were probably safer ways to build its business.

When looking at any activity, innovators always ask the threshold question, "Why?"

If the "Why?" question has no relevant rationale, then the "Why not?" question must follow.

When legendary Notre Dame University football coach Knute Rockne was a player at Notre Dame in 1913, he teamed up with quarterback Gus Dorias and caught a forward pass that helped "The Fightin' Irish" upset a powerhouse Army squad in West Point. Considered one of the very first forward passes ever to be thrown in a college football game...players, officials and fans alike were astonished. After all, this new way to advance the ball seemed risky.

Risky? Yes. Safe? No. Nonetheless, Gus Dorias' pass soared high into the air and was caught by the young Rockne in the end zone. Touchdown!

Everyone was surprised. Was it really a touchdown? Was it insanity? Was it a penalty? Was it progress?

The referees deliberated on the play and considered penalizing Notre Dame, however, there were no rules prohibiting the forward pass. In fact, in 1906, the Collegiate Rules Committee agreed that the forward pass, though "...a very risky offensive maneuver," was an acceptable form of offense.

Ironically enough, for the first time all afternoon, fans were energized and excited by this new way to "gain ground." They were surprised, confused, taken aback...but excited nonetheless.

Today, now that the forward pass is both acceptable offensive behavior and a mainstay of so many college and professional football attack plans, I venture to say most fans would agree that the game could get very boring without a good share of passes going up in the air. What was once unorthodox and seemingly illegal has become the tactical flame that rekindled interest and excitement in modern day football.

Rockne helped redefine the rules of football offense. He was clearly an innovator. He certainly didn't "play it safe."

———◇———

**Innovators always energize, excite and
find new ways to "gain ground."
Redefinition is an important ingredient in innovation.**

———◇———

Don't penalize the fans! Don't penalize customers. Rules were made to be broken...or at least reevaluated.

Still, convincing others to accept the forward pass wasn't easy. Changes never are. After years of debate and deliberation, the organization that governed the sport of college football in its early years (1920s) agreed that the forward pass was "risky" but acceptable. They decided its benefit was speeding up what then was a slow game and concluded that the forward pass might bring new excitement to the sport.

And so, what started as a possible penalty ended up as progress. I can't imagine what modern day football would be today without the forward pass. Can you?

Through it all, however, there are those who disagree with breaking (or reinventing) rules in favor of even the most calculated risks. Case in point, University of Texas football coach Darryl Royal was very negative about "the forward pass" and once said, "There are only three things that can happen when you throw a pass...and two of them are bad!"

Business people who constantly question, who constantly ask "Why?" invariably grow, succeed, innovate and prosper.

———◇———

There is tremendous value in not only answering questions but also in questioning answers.

———◇———

Challenging and perhaps even breaking rules simply accelerate the growth process. It represents expansion and a way to raise the bar on activities and ultimately accomplishment. Breaking rules may not be "safe," however, when appropriate they may very well be necessary ingredients for growth and progress.

Music, pre-Beatles, was marked by lyrics that had absolutely no meaning. For instance, a typical song refrain might have been, "Tell your ma. Tell your pa. Our love is goin' to grow. Ooh-wah!"

Rock n' Rollers at the time were disheveled and unkempt. They wore dirty jeans (then called "dungarees"), open shirts exposing what chest hair the young artists might have had and they always turned and pointed their collars up. They had pompadour hairdos with what was called a "DA" (Duck's Ass) on the back of their hairline.

Then came John, Paul, George and Ringo dressed in black suits, wearing white shirts and ties. Their hair was neatly cropped and they emphasized both musical quality and meaningful words.

They broke the rules.

By doing so, they created new rules and a new musical style.

Also in music, Bob Dylan changed the face of folk music when he appeared at The Newport (Rhode Island) Folk Festival in 1965 playing an electric guitar instead of the traditional folk acoustic guitar. Many traditional folk music fans "booed" the bard while the "undecideds" eventually became fans of the new genre he created, named "folk rock."

Coffee was a traditional beverage that was primarily marketed in a sleepy fashion on supermarket shelves. Starbucks came along and presented consumers with theater, aroma and great visual in-store décor packages that made the coffee shop (usually referred to as a "shoppe") a business phenomenon.

They took coffee off the supermarket shelves and put it on street corners, in carts, in kiosks, in airports, on college campuses, in hotels and more. Starbucks rewrote the rules.

Retailing's "category killers" such as Home Depot, Blockbuster Video, PetSmart and Toys 'R' Us all broke the rules, and in doing so, created new industries...and thrived.

Marie's Bleu Cheese Salad Dressing, after a long, long uphill battle, eventually convinced supermarket operators that salad dressing should be marketed, positioned and placed in the produce section next to lettuce. Now that seems logical, doesn't it?

Still, grocers all around the U.S. initially refused to place Marie's products in the produce section of their grocery stores.

We can only imagine a closed-minded retailer saying to the Marie's sales representative, "What are you crazy? What are you nuts? Putting salad dressing next to lettuce in my produce department is insane. What are you idiots? It's not the way we do things around here!"

Why was this so difficult for supermarkets to accept?

I guess it had something to do with the "Commandments."

Didn't God give Moses "Eleven Commandments?" You know, the first ten were the ones we memorized when we were kids and the "Eleventh Commandment" stated "Salad dressing must be marketed on aisle seven...never in the produce department. That's the way we've always done it around here."

Through it all, Marie's persevered. Eventually finding a grocer that placed their salad dressing in its produce department, both grocer and Marie's made an interesting discovery. Salad dressing sold great when positioned next to lettuce.

Word traveled fast and soon retailers all over the United States jumped on the Marie's Bleu Cheese bandwagon. After a high-speed year building national distribution, Marie's became America's

"No. 1 selling bleu cheese salad dressing" and has not relinquished that position since.

———◇———

There is obviously only one immutable rule in
business development and that one rule is:
"There are no rules!" (Nor should there be.)

———◇———

- Fashion knows no rules.
- Innovation breaks all rules.
- Visionaries see through rules.

A collector of quotations (most without source information, unfortunately), I'm often reminded of the following as related to rules.

"Those who say it can't be done need to get out of the way of those who are doing it!"

As well as avoiding the myth that suggests "playing it safe," as stated earlier, we should also ignore the related myth that asserts "we need permission!"

For whatever reason, America believes it needs permission.

McDonald's hasn't given us permission to order a Big Mac, Fries and Coke before 10:30 a.m. It wasn't until 1983 that most U.S. cities granted us permission to make a right turn on a red light.

How many times have we all heard, "Are we permitted to do that?" or "Are we permitted to do it that way?"

Business building requires boldness. Don't necessarily play it safe and don't feel like you must ask for permission.

Management needs to reward more employees for disturbing the peace and questioning everything. Questioning leads to education, enlightenment and understanding. In addition, it's imperative that we accept the fact that the ultimate answers we might receive could very well contradict our old rules, as well as the safe way to do things.

Playing it safe is playing without risk. Over and over we've heard the reluctant ask, "What is the risk we're taking if we do this?" when in reality, if growth is the goal, they should instead be asking, "What is the risk we're taking if we don't do this?"

Playing it safe "might" provide for small incremental growth. However, taking risk and breaking rules, in a well-planned, calculated manner, can lead to quantum leap growth. In the words of legendary New York Yankee manager, Casey Stengal, "You can't steal second with your foot on first."

Whether it's risk on the base-path or risk in business, the ends must justify the means. In other words, the risk-reward ratio should be analyzed carefully and needs to make sense.

Through it all, if one truly targets quantum leap growth as opposed to incremental step-by-step expansion, there must be both an inclination to take chances as well as a willingness to accept potential failure. Clearly, the more chances one takes, the more opportunities there are for different degrees of both success and of course, failure.

THE BENEFIT OF FAILURE

In reality, however, failure can be an invaluable part of the growth process provided we learn from the experience and apply those learnings to our advantage in future initiatives.

The best example I know of this comes in a quick historical review of Abraham's Lincoln's road to The White House:

- He failed in business in 1831.
- He was defeated for the Legislature in 1832.
- He had a second business bankruptcy in 1833.
- He suffered a nervous breakdown in 1836.
- He was defeated for Speaker of the Illinois House in 1838.
- He was defeated for Elector of the Illinois Senate in 1840.
- He was defeated for the U.S. Congress in 1843.
- He was again defeated for the U.S. Congress in 1848.
- He was defeated for the U.S. Senate in 1855.
- He was defeated for U.S. Vice President in 1856.
- He was defeated, the second time, for the U.S. Senate in 1858.
- He was *elected* President in 1860.

When he was finally elected President, "Honest Abe" told newspaper reporters that the most important education received in his life were those lessons learned through "trials, tribulations, as well as both business and political failures."

Sometimes success is a "game of chance." In order to quantum leap productivity and achievement, we may have to avoid safety zones and simply "go for it." There comes a time in every tightrope walker's life when they work without a net. Even little children eventually take the training wheels off their bicycles.

Progress is all about choices. You know, do I pursue "X" or do I pursue "Y?" That certainly seems like the safe way to approach an opportunity, however, let's not forget the intense power derived from wanting it all and trying it all. Some have referred to this as the "power of and..." *In other words, why should we have to consider one "or" another choice? Why can't we consider one "and" the other choice...you know, grab it all? Why not have our cake and eat it...why not both?*

The question always arises, "What about focus?"

My response: "What about expanded focus?"

I, personally, like the "want it all, try it all" position.

Yes, career and business building are both games of chance. That's why analyzing the "risk-reward ratio" is important (the greater the risk, the greater the reward). I personally find it exciting to review the many challenges, chances, and choices available. They're all opportunities.

When singing about an opportunity, singer-songwriter Dan Fogelberg wrote, "It's a chance of a lifetime, in a lifetime of chance."

We are truly living an ongoing "lifetime of chance" and choice.

> So Wilbur. Hey Orville. Are you guys nuts?
> If God wanted man to fly, he'd put wings
> on his body instead of arms.

If we take a chance, we, too, might soar with the eagles.

Challenge the Myths of Your Own Conventional Wisdom...

CHAPTER HIGHLIGHTS

- It's human nature to come up with all the reasons why something can't be done, as opposed to coming up with all the reasons something can be done.

- History books are filled with important stories of great achievements performed by visionaries who defied the rules and ignored the "play it safe" myth.

- It's no small wonder that so many business people avoid making decisions, can't make decisions or desperately need "permission" to act.

- Permission is a lever. When it comes to levers, I say "pull...or be pulled!" If in doubt, do!

- The fact is that traditional ways of doing things become outdated.

- Innovators always energize, excite and find new ways to "gain ground." Redefinition is an important ingredient in innovation.

- Business people who constantly question, who constantly ask "Why?" invariably grow, succeed, innovate and prosper.

- There is tremendous value in not only answering questions but also questioning answers.

- Challenging and perhaps even breaking rules simply accelerate the growth process. It represents expansion and a way to raise the bar on activities and ultimately accomplishment. Breaking rules may not be "safe," however, when appropriate they may very well be necessary ingredients for growth and progress.

- There is a time for evolution and a time for revolution.

- There is obviously only one immutable rule in business development and that one rule is "There are no rules!" (nor should there be any)

- Those who say it can't be done need to get out of the way of those who are doing it!

- For whatever reason, America believes it needs permission.

- Business building requires boldness. Don't necessarily play it safe and don't feel like you must ask for permission.

- Management needs to reward more employees for disturbing the peace and questioning everything.

- If one truly targets quantum leap growth as opposed to incremental step-by-step expansion, there must be both an inclination to take chances as well as a willingness to accept potential failure.

- Failure can be an invaluable part of the growth process provided we learn from the experience and apply those learnings to our advantage in future initiatives.

- Progress is all about choices.

- Why should we have to consider one "or" another choice? Why can't we consider one "and" the other choice...you know, grab it all? Why not have our cake and eat it...why not both?

- The question always arises, "What about focus? My response..." What about expanded focus?" I, personally, like the "want it all, try it all" positioning.

◇

MYTH FOURTEEN

TIME IS ON OUR SIDE

"Golden Girl" actress Mae West altered the old quotation, "He who hesitates is lost" to what I find to be a more appropriate and important quote, "He who hesitates is last!"

When you consider the fact that today we have an incredible array and assortment of modern conveniences and technological advances, one would assume that these time-saving devices actually provide us with "extra time."

Okay, readers, if you have a microwave oven, raise your hand. (C'mon, participate. Don't be apathetic. Hey, you bought the book. Participate. Stretch a little. You've been reading too long.)

If you have an electric garage door opener, raise your hand.

If you have a remote control television set, raise your hand.

If you have "spare time," now raise your hand. (I don't see any. I don't see any hands up.)

Although we have the opportunity to own, rent, or borrow all the modern, high-tech, efficient and convenient "time-saver" equipment designed to make our lives easier, the reality is that "time-savers" truly don't save us time. We fill up time gaps and spaces quickly with some other activity, some other task. Invariably, we always have a whole lot "more to do."

WE ARE A SOCIETY THAT IS ACTIVITY AND TECHNOLOGY RICH—BUT TIME POOR!

It is precisely because of being "time poor" that we *must* dedicate ourselves and our businesses to being efficient opportunists who never let proverbial "grass grow under our feet."

I love rock n' roll's Rolling Stones, however, I always smile when Mick Jagger sings, "Time is on our side...yes it is!"

Time is not "on our side." No it isn't...or more poetically, no it ain't!

When a business colleague tells me, "We have time," I reply, "No way! Foul! Myth! Myth!"

The clock is every business person's enemy.

Time will continue to grow as the important currency in both our lives and our enterprises. "Save me time and I'll love you forever, even if the convenience offered costs me a little more!"

Consider that the pre-sliced and diced bagged lettuce on supermarket produce department shelves costs, on average, $2.59 a bag, while a raw, uncut traditional head of lettuce in the same department costs somewhere between $.69 and $1.29. The diced and sliced value-added produce is blowing off the shelves, selling incredibly well. Yet, the product costs more and oh, by the way, pack for pack, offers the consumer less total yield than the unadulterated, untouched standard head of lettuce.

It's all about time (and convenience)!

Mae was right. If you hesitate on an opportunity, you surely will be last.

You would think that with virtually every adult wearing a timepiece on their wrist as an ever-present, constant reminder of the passage of time that we would be more frugal and protective of our time...and make the most of all opportunities. I find it ironic that in so many of the business meetings I attend, I've observed associate after associate repeatedly glance at their watches, yet, few do little to speed up the meeting, or bring a runaway meeting back into focus, or even try to efficiently establish action steps and closure to a off-schedule meeting...etc.

Time contracts are constantly being broken.

Wristwatches should serve as a constant reminder of time's passage.

I smile when I recall a boring Botany class I took at the University of Maryland and a quick reaction by one of my classmates during an incredibly long, dull lecture on pistils and stamens. Our Professor, Ralph Tedia (we called him "Tedious"), noticed my pal Paul Bodner constantly staring at his watch—obviously counting down the minutes until class dismissal.

Professor "Tedious" interrupted his own lecture, turned to my buddy "Bod" and asked, "Mr. Bodner, will you kindly tell me why you seem to be looking at your watch so often?"

Ever quick, Paul replied, "Yes sir! I was afraid, sir, that you wouldn't have time to finish your interesting lecture."

————◇————

We stare at the clock, live by the clock, yet, we waste
so much time and miss so many opportunities.

————◇————

One reason this occurs is that the art of brutal, candid honesty and the use of the "No" word are difficult competencies to master.

Why is "No" such a difficult word to say and such an impossible concept to grasp?

Why do we often feel guilty when we say "No?"

Psychologists claim it has a lot to do with man's obsessive need to be liked, loved and cared about. After all, everyone wants to be important and appreciated.

The threshold question is, however, what price are we paying for delivering too many "Yes" responses? Every "Yes" and every commitment means extending, distributing and giving up more seconds, minutes, hours, days, weeks, months, etc.

Shakespeare said, "We burn daylight."

Some business opportunities open and close very quickly. Flexibility, and more importantly, agility are critical to capitalizing on those high-growth quick-openers that knock on our office and company doors. If a corporate culture is more oriented toward a wait-and-see posture, then too many business building opportunities will fly by and be grabbed by the competition.

How, then, does a company (and culture) that is more inclined toward *slow than go* alter its behavior patterns and become quicker to respond to time-sensitive opportunities?

The first major change a company must agree to is the absolute acceptance that every day brings forth new chances, challenges, choices and a boatload filled with new opportunities. Looking back and dwelling on the near or distant past shouldn't be part of a company's culture if it "truly" desires to become more opportunistic.

———◇———

**Look ahead. Look up. Embrace each new day
as one that brings new opportunities.**

———◇———

That great sage, Anonymous, once said, "Art is long, life short; judgment difficult and opportunity transient."

The transient nature of most opportunities makes it a compelling imperative that the second strategy for changing corporate culture and efficiently capitalizing on time sensitive chances is the building of company policies, procedures, standards, processes and practices oriented toward "quick close" action.

Simply put, developing a process for quickly identifying, qualifying and attacking opportunities, and making those opportunities a priority is an absolute "must."

Mom used to tell me, "There's no time like the present." I laugh at that advice these days because I'm so time poor that I think a more meaningful idea for my life, lifestyle and life-speed is "There's no present like more time!"

A third strategy is the development of a corporate culture that includes "fear" as one of its driving forces.

Fear can be an extraordinary motivator to get things done...to capitalize on time sensitive programs...to be more efficient...to react quicker...and to jump on an opportunity faster than the competition.

If you've ever been chased by a growling, snarling dog, you will know exactly what I mean when I say "fear is great motivator."

I can only imagine how the U.S. Olympic sprint team would race if every runner had an angry Doberman Pincher or German Shepherd lunging at them at the starting block and chasing them for the duration of the race. We're talking world records here, folks.

Fear can be an enormous driver of reaction, speed and action. In fact, conqueror Napoleon was said to believe that there were only two things that "moved men"...self-interest and fear.

Whether it be developing a strategy to embrace each new day as one bringing forth new business development prospects...or working to create a culture and process for capitalizing on time-sensitive opportunities...or instigating a feeling of fear (What will happen if we don't jump on this opportunity quickly?)...successful companies (and careers) manage time.

I personally find the whole concept of "time" and "opportunity" intriguing.

Whenever an associate, employee, friend or even a family member bemoans the tragedy of having too little time to accomplish anything or not enough time to be productive, I think of busy Ben Franklin.

In a period of about fifteen short years, he invented the stove, bifocal glasses, copper roofs, a damper for chimneys, a "grab it" pole for pulling items off high retail shelves and was instrumental in early tests of electrical power. Franklin did experiments that proved the color white was the coolest garment color to wear in summer and he was also responsible for paving and lighting the streets of Philadelphia. He invented a piece of furniture that was both chair and stepstool, created America's first fire company, formed the first U.S. lending library, founded the "dead letter" office at the postal service and wrote position papers on how nice it would be to have trees bordering both sides of main streets, an idea that he eventually implemented with friends in colonial Philadelphia.

These accomplishments represent just a handful of his work. Oh yes, he did all this while publishing a weekly newspaper and running five different businesses.

He was a statesman, a politician, a journalist, a scientist and a pioneer in education when he founded and served as the first president of one of America's oldest universities, the University of Pennsylvania.

Franklin's amazing credentials go on and on and on.

This was a busy guy who obviously mastered the effective management of time.

However, the key learning is simple and best conveyed through Ben Franklin's very own words of wisdom, "Never put off till tomorrow that which you can do today!"

In June 1985, Bill Gates suggested that Apple Computers consider licensing the rights to develop Mac compatible computer systems to other companies. John Scully, then Apple's CEO, didn't believe *the time was right*. Today, most industry observers are convinced that had Apple licensed its operating system to outside technology companies (perhaps even Microsoft), it would have ultimately avoided the severe financial problems it experienced in 1996. *Timing is everything!*

Think about those companies and individuals that were agile and fast enough to jump all over time-sensitive opportunities and turn each into huge business building windfalls. The early investors in Nike, Microsoft and Home Depot all made fortunes. Timing is everything!

It's not surprising that shortly after Michael Jordan and his Chicago Bulls won their fifth NBA championship in 1996 and "MJ" became, perhaps, the most famous, highly visible sports celebrity in history, that "opportunists" like Nike, Quaker Oats, Sara Lee and Warner Brothers jumped all over this "quick-opener" to market Jordan tie-ins, products, endorsements and even businesses.

Nike announced an unprecedented move to create and develop a special company, an autonomous profit center and subsidiary of Nike, that would be presided over by Michael himself. In a day and age where celebrity endorsements are commonplace, Nike "raised the bar," so to speak, and moved from a typical endorsement agreement to actually partnering with number "23" and developing a new company for and with Michael Jordan (an autonomous division of Nike, Inc.). Nike seized the moment (and opportunity).

The Quaker Oats Company extended Jordan's contract as spokesperson for their Gatorade division and Sara Lee "inked" a long-term contract with Jordan to continue strutting around on television commercials promoting Hanes underwear, as well as other Sara Lee products.

Warner Brothers came out with their "Space Jam" movie that saw Michael Jordan co-star with cartoon legends Bugs Bunny, Elmer Fudd, Daffy Duck and others.

That's not all, folks!

The list of businesses, products, programs and co-ventures that now include Jordan are long. Why? Simply put, a handful of smart business people recognized the "Jordan" brand as one offering an alliance opportunity too good to pass up. They also understood that as well as being viable, the Jordan window of opportunity was likely to be time sensitive. On the other side of the contract, Michael Jordan and his business advisors couldn't afford wasting time either...not with opportunities barreling in so rapidly and Jordan's fame skyrocketing. After all, Jordan's name, face, reputation, charisma and brand recognition were hot commodities.

There was obviously no time to waste. Any business that tabled discussions for "another day and another time" lost the Jordan opportunity.

Hesitate and be last!

The state of the American consumer in the early 1990s made the time for Starbucks to emerge exactly right.

Consider these consumer snapshots.

- Consumers were dizzy, busy, hassled and harried.
- Consumers were activity rich and time poor.
- Consumers lived in a "culture of convenience."
- Consumers were becoming generally older (the "graying" of America).
- Consumers needed to escape and grab infrequent opportunities to decompress and relax. Why? The pace of life and living was intense.
- Consumers grew to becoming very flavor oriented and conscious.
- Consumers wanted the "real thing." Imitations and perceived imitations weren't acceptable.

Along came the kids from Seattle.

Starbucks jumped all over these consumer trends, capitalized on the opportunities and timed their frontal attack perfectly.

Consumers voted for Starbucks with their dollars because it fit their "need states" to a "T" (actually to a "coffee"). Their products, programs and marketing premise came at precisely the right time for consumers.

In 1993, I facilitated a focus group sponsored by a large coffee manufacturer. Its objective was to better understand the Starbucks phenomenon. The following write-up represents a compilation of remarks and conclusions taken from this session.

> To a dizzy, busy, hassled and harried person, a piping hot cup of delicious, flavorful coffee (love that Mocha Java) is perfect to take the edge off one's day. Being "time poor" and "convenience driven," consumers are thrilled that Starbucks stores, kiosks and carts are now appearing everywhere...in malls, on street corners, on college campuses, in airports, in stadiums, even on airplanes. And older consumers, coffee lovers from a rich, deep American coffee drinking tradition, welcome the renewed interest in coffee and readily accept new age coffee flavors. Funny, the lion share of the population being older means there are probably lots and lots of real coffee lovers out there. The marketplace is broad. Also, busy consumers welcome the opportunity to just slow down, decompress and relax with a cup of Starbucks Coffee in their hands. Ah yes, the stuff isn't artificial, soluble or instant. It's the real thing. Starbucks roasts those beans right in front of the consumer's eyes.

This compilation and blending of remarks could have been written by Starbucks for ad copy. It wasn't. It represented about a dozen consumer viewpoints. After all, when consumers are satisfied, they themselves tend to write the best ad copy and become wonderful product ambassadors.

Consumer-focused and market-driven, it was the right time for Starbucks. And timing is everything!

History books are filled with stories of companies and people who realized that the efficient, effective use and management of time surely can lead to competitive advantage. There is also a long list of companies who sadly enough have said, "If I only would have..." or "You know, we really should have..."

- Hindsight is 20/20.
- Time definitely is not on our side.
- Time is the enemy.

However, through foresight, insight, spirit, vision, wisdom, logic and lots of energy, time can be controlled and conquered. We can capitalize on opportunities.

It's about time!

Challenge the Myths of
Your Own Conventional Wisdom...

CHAPTER HIGHLIGHTS

- He who hesitates is last!
- Time-savers truly don't save us time.
- We are a society that is activity and technology rich...but time poor!
- The clock is every business person's enemy.
- Although we stare at the clock and live by the clock, with intense, constant focus on clocks, we still waste so much time and miss so many opportunities.
- We often feel guilty when we say "no."
- The threshold question is, however, what price are we paying for delivering too many "yes" responses?
- Look ahead. Look up. Embrace each new day as one that brings new opportunities.
- Simply put, developing a process for quickly identifying, qualifying and attacking opportunities, and making those opportunities a priority is an absolute "must."
- Fear is a great motivator.
- Timing is everything.
- Hindsight is 20/20.
- Time definitely is not on our side.
- Want to optimize business opportunities? It's about time!

◇

COMMENCEMENT

I was always intrigued by the name given the closing ritual at a school graduation ceremony.

Commencement?

Commencement!

Hmmm...according to my companion, Daniel Webster, "commencement" is defined as "a start," as "a beginning." I just couldn't figure out why "a start" and "a beginning" would come at the conclusion, the closure, the end of four years of high school, college or some other academic pilgrimage. Why didn't they call the service the "culmination exercises," "the grand finale" or some other finish-line oriented name?

I found it puzzling until I, myself, started graduating from a school, or two, and heard a few commencement speeches directed at me. In fact, in my quest to learn more about "commencement," my son, Eric, gave me a marvelous book called *Hold Fast Your Dreams*,[23] a collection of commencement speeches...with messages shared by the likes of Arthur Ashe, Jimmy Carter, Cathy Guisewite, Billy Joel, Colin Powell, Dr. Seuss and others. I really got into this "commencement" thing.

I eventually understood. You see, regardless of what mountain you've been climbing, what challenges you've been facing, what journey you've been traveling, and in this case, what book you've been reading...adventurers who care and dare to conquer, learn and excel never come to the "end." Because of their energy, spirit and insatiable appetite for education, adventurers are awarded a lifetime supply of commencement exercises.

Whether it's beginning a new initiative, campaign, entrepreneurial venture, job, career or position...spirited people embrace commencement...over and over again.

It's another start...another "new leaf"...another chance...another wonderful, terrific opportunity to make a difference.

I once received an award in college for a poem I wrote entitled, "I Love New Year's Eve. I Must Be New Year's Adam." I'm certain it would never have make *The Saturday Review of Literature* but my point was simple. *Every new year brings new challenges, new choices, new life, another chance....and another bucket of opportunities.*

That's why I love New Year's Eve so much. It's another shot, folks!

It's the way of our natural world. Regardless of how terrible the weather is on Wednesday...come Thursday or Friday or Saturday or one day soon, the sun will shine again. That's the beauty of life...and business!

If you blow an assignment, miss a deadline, lose a sale, botch up an order, fall short of an objective or screw up BIG TIME...there's always another chance, another opportunity, another commencement exercise.

The three keys to unlocking the magic commencement treasure box filled with new opportunities for reinvention, revitalization, reinvigoration and another new "start" and "beginning" are:

- Energy
- Optimism
- Education

Although I sincerely hope this book has provided you with the impetus to generate energy in your business life, as well as cause for becoming more optimistic about future opportunities, *energy* and *optimism* are keys you're going to have to find and nurture yourself. Those are in your court. They are self-developed.

On the other hand, the *education* piece is one I hope I've helped you with through the pages of my book, *Ready, Blame, Fire!*

My commencement address to you is short, succinct and to the point:

Don't fall into the common trap of believing the many myths of marketing and business that, by tradition, have been respected and revered for too many years...because that's the way things have always been done (and seen).

Rules come and go. Question everything!

I hope you now see (and agree) that bigger isn't necessarily better...and the first one "in" doesn't always win...and that close enough is no longer good enough...and that it could "happen here"...and "the best offense isn't necessarily a good defense..." and on and on and on...

A neat little trick and reminder to help you remember the messages of these myths might be through a parody title of that traditional song, *Here She Comes, Myth America!* Cute, huh? Hum it, sing it and remember not to fall prey to business-stifling myths.

Review the "misses." There's no shame in making a mistake. There should be lots of shame, however, if you make the same mistake twice...or if you're provided a barrel full of example mistakes (misses) and you don't learn from past blunders.

Eastern Airlines is gone. Howard Johnson's barely has a pulse. IBM lost billions of dollars. Woolworth closed its doors. Ford's Edsel was a fiasco. Euro-Disney got fried in France. New Coke was a "classic" mistake. Miss after miss after painful miss...

Listen and learn. Study the past. Proceed with newfound insight on what works and what doesn't work. Learning from past failures can serve as a vital link to succeeding in the future.

Finally, consider the following, my Compelling Imperatives for business building success, which are easily remembered by the word "I.M.P.E.R.A.T.I.V.E.S."

I   *Ideas, Information.* Develop a culture that encourages and fosters new ways of looking at things. Understand that along with quality products and services, we are in a world that moves because of ideas, information and knowledge. Having bigger and better ideas will lead to competitive advantage.

M   *Market-Driven.* Focus on the customer. No longer can an enterprise take the position, "We want to market and sell those products and services we prefer producing." It is now vital to "...market and sell those products and services our customer wants us to produce." Everything a company does must be done because of some customer need or requirement.

P *Planning.* There's a future for those who plan for it. Become obsessed with planning and plan implement-ation. Vision, mission, objectives, barriers to achieving objectives, strategies, tactics and more...Plan, plan, plan!

E *Education.* Every industry has a constant flow of new information, ideas and trends. Success, in the future, will not be in the hands of the "learned." It will be the "learning" who soar. Continuously improve, continuously learn and never forget...education is only power when it is applied.

R *Risk-Taking.* Re-evaluate your viewpoint on "risk." The old risk-oriented question was *What's the risk we're taking if we DO this?* A new way to look at risk comes in the question, *What's the risk we're taking if we DON'T do this?* Take a chance. No guts, no glory. No risk, no reward.

A *Adapt. Adjust.* Change is inevitable. Growth is optional. The Brontosaurus, as well as many corporate dinosaurs, all went from distinction to extinction because they failed to adapt and adjust to change.

T *Technology. Embrace* technology. It's here, it's real and it's vitally important. Techno-peasants will fall behind.

I *Implementation.* Great ideas are often unsuccessful because of poor implementation and execution. It's amazing to consider how many sound ideas have been trashed not because of the ideas, but because of substandard execution. Ideas are easy. Effective implementation is the challenge.

V *Value.* Focus your business development activities on the constant creation of new value for your clients, customers and consumers. Value should be defined as *exceeding expectations.*

E *Extra*! The difference between ordinary and EXTRAordinary is that little "extra." Constantly strive to provide customers "extra" value and benefits. Sam Walton said, "Strive to get extraordinary results from ordinary people." Provide "Extra, Extra!" and the world will read all about it.

S *Strategic Alliances.* There's surely strength in numbers. Seek symbiotic relationships. Search for synergies.

Network like crazy. Value, efficiency and growth are the key benefits derived from joint ventures and alliances.

Well, you've finished my book and graduated.

Hopefully, it didn't take you four painful years...nor a Guido Sarducci inspired five minutes.

Although I respect Nike for all they have accomplished, I believe there's a necessary add-on word that should be applied to their motto, "Just do it!"

You see, if you "just do it," you might do it wrong.

Therefore, I recommend that "Just do it...right!" is the way we should approach both our lives and businesses.

Doing it "right" is a byproduct of a complex mixture of ideas, information, education, actionable data, motivation, inspiration, perspiration, challenging conventional wisdom, learning from the past and constantly creating a new future.

So many of us deceive and convince ourselves that we're energetic, we're innovative, we're forever learning, we're spirited and that we are obsessed with just doing it right. In reality, many of us truly aren't.

Don't give it all "lip service." Don't play the game "Emperor's New Clothes." Be honest with yourself. Rise to the occasion...care and dare to be great. Go for it, but go for it right!

A man named William D. Wintle once played football for the legendary University of Alabama coach, Paul "Bear" Bryant. Wintle didn't play much but was an inspirational team member nonetheless. A terrific writer, Bill Wintle, wrote a marvelous poem for his coach called *The Man In The Glass.*

Bryant loved the poem so much that before an Orange Bowl game, as the story goes, he passed out copies of the poem, along with a small ladies' compact mirror, to all his "Crimson Tide" players. He told his team something to the effect of, "At the end of this game, actually at the end of every one of life's games you play, go to a mirror and look yourselves squarely in the eyes. If you can honestly tell yourself that you worked your hardest, committed yourself to excellence and played your very best...regardless of what the scoreboard numbers say...you're a winner!"

In closing this Commencement chapter, here's W.D. Wintle's poem as a present and keepsake for you to constantly review and reread (as I do). Never forget "the man in the glass." Just do it...right!

THE MAN IN THE GLASS

When you get what you want in your struggle through life
and the world makes you king for a day
just go to the mirror and look at yourself
and see what that man has to say.
For it isn't your father, your mother, or wife
whose judgment on you must pass.
The one whose verdict counts most in your life
is the man starring back from the glass.
You may be like Jack Horner and chisel a plum
and think you're a wonderful guy.
But the man in the glass says you're only a bum
if you can't look him straight in the eye.
You may go through life and
get pats on the back as you pass.
But your final reward will be heartaches and tears,
if you've cheated the man in the glass.

—W.D. Wintle

Go make a difference!
Commence!

Challenge the Myths of
Your Own Conventional Wisdom...

CHAPTER HIGHLIGHTS

- Regardless of what mountain you've been climbing, what challenges you've been facing, what journey you've been traveling, and in this case, what book you've been reading...adventurers who care and dare to conquer, learn and excel never come to the "end." Because of their energy, spirit and insatiable appetite for education, adventurers are awarded a lifetime supply of commencement exercises.

- Every new year brings new challenges, new choices, new life, another chance...and another bucket of opportunities.
- The three keys to unlocking the magic commencement treasure box filled with new opportunities for reinvention, revitalization, reinvigoration and another new beginning are:
  1. Energy
  2. Optimism
  3. Education
- Commencement suggestions:
  - ◇ Don't fall into the common trap of believing the many "myths" of marketing. Rules come and go. Question everything!
  - ◇ Review the "misses." There's no shame in making a mistake. There should be lots of shame, however, if you make the same mistake twice. Listen and learn. Study the past.
  - ◇ Utilize the following "compelling imperatives" for business building success.

    I   *Ideas, Information*–Develop a culture that encourages and fosters new ways of looking at things.

    M   *Market-Driven*–Everything a company does must be done because of some customer need or requirement.

    P   *Planning*–There's a future for those who plan for it.

    E   *Education*–Continuously improve. Continuously learn. When you're through learning, you're through.

    R   *Risk-Taking*–Re-evaluate your viewpoint on "risk." Take a chance. No guts, no glory. No risk, no reward.

    A   *Adapt, Adjust*–Change is inevitable. Growth is optional.

    T   *Technology*–Embrace technology. Techno-peasants will fall behind.

    I   *Implementation*–Ideas are easy. Effective implemen-tation is the challenge.

    V   *Value*–Value should be defined as "exceeding expec-tations."

    E   *Extra, Extra!*–The difference between ordinary and EXTRAordinary is that little "extra."

    S   *Strategic Alliances*–There's strength in numbers.
- Rise to the occasion...care and dare to be great.

- Just do it...right!
- Go make a difference!

◇

REFERENCES

1. Dylan, Bob. "The Times They Are A-Changin'." 1963, 1964 Warner Bros. Music, 1991 renewed by Special Rider Music.

2. Barker, Joel Arthur. *Paradigms: The Business of Discovering the Future*. New York: HarperBusiness, 1993, 140. (Note: The term "Paradigm Pioneer®" that appears on page 6 in *Ready, Blame, Fire!* is from Joel Arthur Barker's book herewith referenced.)

3. Reprinted by permission of Warner Books, Inc. from *A Whack On the Side of the Head* by Roger Von Oech. Copyright © 1990 by Roger Von Oech. All rights reserved.

4. Longfellow, Henry Wadsworth. *The Political Works of Henry Wadsworth Longfellow*. Boston: Houghton Mifflin Co., 1975, p.207.

5. Walton, Sam and John Huey. *Sam Walton, Made In America*. New York: Doubleday, 1992.

6. Day, Doris. "Que Sera, Sera." Jay Livingston and St. Angelo Music, 1955.

7. Orwell, George. *1984*. New York: Harcourt Brace & Co., 1982.

8. Chandler, Len. "Keep On Keepin' On." Darhe Music, 1963, 1991.

9. When the Wal*Mart name appears with a star rather than a hypen, it means that store is a Super Center.

10. Frost, Robert. *Robert Frost: Collected Poems, Prose & Plays*. New York: Library Classics of the United States, 1996, p. 47.

11. Pritchett, Price. *You²: A High-Velocity Formula for Multiplying Your Personal Effectiveness in Quantum Leaps*. Dallas: Pritchett & Associates, 1990.

12. Fisher, Anne B. "Corporate Reputations." *Fortune*. 4 March 1996: 96.

13. Grayson, Jr., C. Jackson and Carla O'Dell. *American Business, A Two Minute Warning: Ten Changes Managers Must Make to Survive Into the 21st Century*. New York: The Free Press, 1987.

14. Reese, Jennifer. "America's Most Admired Corporations." *Fortune*. 8 Feb. 1993: 44-53; Welsh, Tricia. "Best and Worst Corporate

Reputations." *Fortune.* 7 Feb. 1994: 58-66.; Jacob, Rahul. "Corporate Reputations." *Fortune.* 6 March 1995: 54-64; Fisher, Anne B. "Corporate Reputations." 4 March 1996: 90-98.

15. Frost, pp. 39-40.

16. "Annie Hall." United Artists, 1977.

17. Food Marketing Institute, 800 Connecticut Ave. NW, Washington, DC 20006

18. U.S. Public Health Service. *Smoking and Health: Report of the Advisory Committee to the Surgeon General of the Public Health Service.* Washington, DC: U.S. Dept. of Health, Education, and Welfare, 1964. 387.

19. Hill, Doug and Jeff Weingrad. *Saturday Night: A Backstage History of SNL.* New York: Beech Tree Books, 1986.

20. Carroll, Lewis. *Alice In Wonderland.* New York: W.W. Norton and Co., 1992.

21. Hardwick, Michael. *The Drake Guide To Gilbert and Sullivan.* New York: Drake Publishers, 1973, p. 149.

22. "Annie Hall."

23. Boyko, Carrie and Kimberly Colen. *Hold Fast Your Dreams.* New York: Scholastic, 1996.

◇

SUGGESTED READINGS

Barker, Joel Arthur. *Paradigms: The Business of Discovering the Future.* New York: Harper Business, 1993.

Blanchard, Kenneth and Spencer Johnson. *The One Minute Manager.* New York: William Morrow, 1982.

Cain, Herman. *Leadership Is Common Sense.* New York: Von Nostrand Reinhold, 1997.

Grayson, Jr., C. Jackson and Carla O'Dell. *American Business, A Two-Minute Warning: Ten Changes Managers Must Make to Survive Into the 21st Century.* New York: The Free Press, 1987.

Kriegel, Robert. *If It Ain't Broke...Break It!* New York: Warner Books, 1991.

Miller, Lawrence. *Barbarians to Bureaucrats.* New York: Fawcett Columbine, 1989.

Peters, Tom. *The Pursuit of Wow!* New York: Vintage Books, 1994.

Pritchett, Price. *You^2: A High-Velocity Formula for Multiplying Your Personal Effectiveness in Quantum Leaps.* Dallas: Pritchett & Associates, 1990.

Smith, Hedrick. *Rethinking America.* New York: Random House, 1995.

Suzaki, Kiyoshi. *The New Manufacturing Challenge.* New York: The Free Press, 1987.

von Oech, Roger. *A Whack On the Side of the Head.* New York: Warner Books, 1990.

Walker, Robert H. *Life In The Age of Enterprise.* New York: Capricorn Books, 1971.

Walton, Sam and John Huey. *Sam Walton, Made In America.* New York: Doubleday, 1992.

Waterman, Robert H. *Adhocracy: The Power To Change.* Knoxville, TN: Whittle Direct Books, 1990.

◇

ABOUT THE AUTHOR

Ira Blumenthal is a business Renaissance man.

The president of CO-OPPORTUNITIES, Inc., an Atlanta-based consulting firm that has counseled world-class clients such as Coca-Cola, Nestle, Exxon, Wal-Mart and others, Blumenthal is an expert in business development, branding and strategic alliances.

He is a visiting instructor at both Michigan State University and the University of Notre Dame.

He has published numerous articles on business development and is the recipient of "The George Washington Honor Medal" for literary excellence, presented by The Freedoms Foundation.

Ira Blumenthal also is a highly successful public speaker who delivers more than 100 speeches annually. His primary topics include "Strategic Alliances," "Business Development," and "Branding." Although his roots are in the food and consumer goods industry, Ira addresses audiences in all industries, both in the United States and abroad (e.g., Australia, Brazil, Canada, France, Great Britain, Mexico). Whether he is speaking to a workshop of fifty people or giving a keynote speech to 5,000, Ira always exceeds expectations, receiving great "grades" from his audiences.

He has received numerous business and civic awards...sits on a number of boards, including the advisory board of Food Chain, a national organization dedicated to feeding the hungry...and is a community activist, as well as little league coach. A former stand-out athlete, early in his career Ira coached college football and lacrosse. In 1998, Ira Blumenthal was named Head Coach of Team USA, leading America's entry in the Seniors Division of the Lacrosse World Cup.

Ready, Blame, Fire! is Ira Blumenthal's first full-length book.

He is married to the former Kim Burgess of Clinton, Missouri. They are the parents of five children: Sharon, Julie, Eric, Jeffrey and Ryan, who keep them very busy and constantly challenged. They live in Atlanta.

As consultant, university instructor, writer, public speaker, community activist and, of course, little league coach, Ira Blumenthal truly is a Renaissance man.

◇